EVOLUTION
AND FAITH

Edited by J.D. Thomas

A·C·U
PRESS
Abilene Christian University Press
Abilene, Texas

Printed in the United States of America.

Book Design, *Ron Hadfield*
Typesetting, *Mel Ristau/Design*

Library of Congress Card Number 87-73028
ACU Press, Abilene, Texas
ISBN 0-915547-99-6

FOREWORD

This volume should help lift the veil of ignorance about evolution and Biblical creation. Its approach is assembled in the writings of eminently qualified men within the religious, scientific, and philosophic communities. The writers are men who have chosen a walk of faith with God and have found a reaffirmation of their faith in the physical realities of the present world.

The men of science who have authored this book are not men who dismiss science in the face of Biblical teachings, or vice versa. They are men of education and experience, recognized by their peers in the scientific community, who have found harmony in nature and philosophy. These students and teachers of the Bible do not depreciate the abilities God has chosen to give us to reason and think and understand, with scientific order, many of the things of this world. You will, perhaps, be startled to discover that creation/evolution is not a choice between faith and fact; it is, rather, a choice between faith and faith.

You will learn what hard, empirical evidence exists and what does not exist. You will be challenged to consider the context and scope of the Genesis account of creation and its affirmation throughout scripture. You will be asked to consider your own view in response to faith and science.

God does not need man to "prove" creation. And nature does not need man's complete understanding to continue to work its wonders. Yet God, the Maker, has seen fit to give us abilities and resources for both faith and science.

God is the Creator of all life. Faith in God stands apart from empirical proof. Yet, science is the extraordinary gift He has given to open grandly the wondrous order of His creation. If you take only bits and pieces from this work, seeking to defend a position, you will be disappointed. Yet, if you will draw on the wisdom of these men, in the entirety of *Evolution and Faith*, you will deepen your understanding and draw closer to the Maker of all things.

William J. Teague
August, 1987

CONTENTS

PREFACE

The issues in the subject of evolution and of its teaching, are very much with us today and are quite relevant to continued discussion. Public ignorance of the history of the tensions between science and religion, of the actual physical facts that relate to evolution, and of the basic philosophical issues involved in it is amazing.

The masses in our society, and probably most among those of the intelligentsia, are merely passive followers of those they consider to be "authorities" in science. The need of the day, therefore, is for people to learn the actual facts and to see the total, broad picture for themselves. Too many of today's decisions concerning the doctrine of evolution are based merely on emotion, not upon facts, and not upon intellect. All of this is justification for this study.

We are thankful to the several authors for their important contributions, and for putting this project ahead of other things in order to get the book out. Gratitude is also owed to many others. To Dr. William J. Teague for advice and support at various stages in the process; to Ron Hadfield and Mel Ristau for design and planning; to Betty Whiteside for a great amount of detailed work and support; and to Terry O'Rear for preparing the Index. Our sincere thanks to all of these.

J. D. Thomas
August, 1987

INTRODUCTION

J. D. T H O M A S

*T*he concern of this book is to consider the truthfulness of the general theory of evolution as it is commonly defined, and to consider what the Christian's attitude should be toward it and toward its impact upon the understanding of the Bible.

There has been a drastic change in the basic philosophical outlook of people in the western world and particularly in America over the past several years. The trend has been toward Naturalism, which means that many people now deny the existence of God and the possibility of supernatural realities. This tendency toward Naturalism as the basic outlook of the average person has come about because of several influences in modern thought:

• The Protestant reformation and the consequent questioning of the concept of an "authority" as the place to get answers;

• The development of the scientific method in problem solving, and an increased appreciation of natural law and its uniform operation;

• The philosophical battle between rationalism and empiricism (sense experience) as the primary way of knowing.

As these tensions were being worked out and the philosophy of Naturalism became more accepted as the basic worldview, there developed a disdain for religious authority and an acceptance of relativism in morality, where the individual decides that his own feelings is the ultimate criterion and authority for what is truth and for what is right and good. This approach means that "every man is the measure of himself," so that many now believe that there are as many different truths as there are individuals, and therefore that there is no absolute, public truth applicable to all people alike. This also includes a rejection of any and all external authority, such as the Bible.

While modern thinkers were busy searching out ways of determining what is truth and what is reality, G.W.F. Hegel (1769-1831) came up with an "evolution of ideas" theory as the way to explain the meaning of history. To him, ideas evolve, in that opposite ideas clash with each other and vie for acceptance (thesis versus antithesis), and then they eventually resolve such tension by the blending of the best of both into a "synthesis," which resulting concept is superior to both of the original ideas and therefore an "upward evolution of ideas" occurs. Hegel's theory held that there was an "entelechy" or some sort of a cosmic force that "pulled" the development of ideas upward towards "ultimate truth." Thus the rise of the concept of a "continuing, straight-line, upward evolution" of both ideas and historical events, came into rather general acceptance because of Hegel's personal dominance of the philosophical scene.

Hegel's concept of an "upward naturalistic evolution" paved the way for Darwin's naturalistic, upward physical evolution of biological life-forms which he set forth in his *Origin of the Species* in 1859. Hegel thus furnished the philosophical background for an immediate acceptance of Darwin's gradual organic evolution of all life-forms, based on "natural selection" and "survival of the fittest." His theory necessarily involves an outright denial of the existence of God and a repudiation of any need for supernatural realities. Langdon Gilkey comments:

> What rescued the 19th century from the despair implicit in Darwinism? It was the fact that quite quickly in scientific and philosophical minds Fate was transformed into a benevolent cosmic Progress. The new secular religion of progressive evolutionism made it possible for Victorian culture, both religious and irreligious, to absorb evolution with truly astounding serenity and speed; believing firmly in inevitable progress, they were able to forget the deeper implications of Darwinism.[1]

It was not long until it was realized that the real problem was "the arrival of the fittest" rather than "the survival of the fittest." It is easy to see that the healthiest, most vigorous organisms could endure and prosper in life better than the less fit, but the question is, "How do newer and better traits and organs get here?" What produces the improvement in life-forms? These questions caused Darwin's theory to weaken greatly until Hugo DeVries about 1900 came up with the concept of mutations. This idea revived the search for a mechanism that hopefully would explain how improved organisms could be brought into existence. This search is still going on for Macro-evolution (between and within the major groupings of creatures) but speciation and variations among the lower levels of organisms have been established.

PROBLEMS FOR THIS STUDY

We wish first to focus attention on the major problems that will be discussed in the study, so that the reader can be alerted to the controversial issues and will be able to watch for them in his reading. We list them numerically for the sake of making definite distinctions:

1. *Definitions:* The General Theory of Evolution — Macro-evolution (All the way from "amoeba to man"), as distinct

from Micro-evolution (Demonstrable minor changes — variations, speciation).

2. *The Authority of Science.* Its realm of expertise, as versus the realm of reality where it cannot speak with any authority. The philosophy of "Scientism."

3. *The Age of the Earth and the Universe.* Whether in the billions of years or in the very few thousands. Valid dating procedures.

4. *Uniformitarianism vs. Catastrophism* as causes of the geological formations. The validity of The Geologic Timetable for dating.

5. *The Flood.* Its actuality. Whether universal or local. Its date. Its impact on geological theory.

6. *Paleontology* and the Fossil remains. The problems of Transitional Fossils and of the Gaps.

7. *What Evolution claims* about the beginning of life on earth, and its development up to the very first fossil forms of which there is any record.

8. *Taxonomy* — The classification of animal forms — from Phyla through Classes, Orders, Families, Genera to Species. To which group does the "kinds" of Genesis 2 apply?

9. *The continuing problem of a Mechanism.* Exactly what caused naturalistic evolution. The problem of extrapolating from mechanisms affecting minor groups to extrapolations affecting major groups.

10. *The Antiquity of Man.* Millions of years or quite recent.

11. *The origin of Mind, Spirit, and Values.* Those faculties of man that distinguish him from the animals.

12. *The change in evolutionary theory* from slow, gradual evolution to rapid changes in order to fit the fossil record. "Punctuated Equilibrium."

13. *The Biblical demands* — What the Bible actually says concerning the Age of the Earth and of Man; about the Flood; about "kinds" of creatures and the possiblity of changes in life forms.

We would remind the reader that this controversy about evolution is really one about whether God exists or not. It is a controversy about whether God or "chance" is responsible for the universe. It argues whether there be any supernatural realities, or whether Nature itself is the "all." Is there a "mind" behind this marvelous universe, which is so logical in all its inner workings and relationships?

We also need to comment on the taxonomic relations of the several creatures of our world. The normally accepted classification of living organisms, on a descending scale, is:

> Phyla
> Classes
> Orders
> Families
> Genera
> Species

Each phylum contains several classes, each class several orders, each order several families, each family several genera, each genus several species. The total number of phyla in the animal kingdom varies from ten to thirty, depending upon the taxonomist doing the classifying. The number of recognized species, at the lower end of the scale, is a million or more, again depending upon the person doing the classifying. Changes among the species, and even the genera are known; but there is no evidence for changes among the phyla or upper groupings of the scale. One would rarely hear the claim that a butterfly and an elephant have common ancestors, but that man is a "brother to a frog" has been claimed.

Philosophy and Evolution

2

EVOLUTION AND THE WAYS OF SCIENCE

ARLIE J. HOOVER

*I*t is bigotry to teach only one theory of origins in the public schools!" That sounds rather modern, doesn't it? You might think it was said just yesterday by a creationist. Actually the statement comes from the year 1925, from the infamous "Monkey Trial" held in Dayton, Tennessee. Clarence Darrow was criticizing the creationist, William Jennings Bryan, for thinking that creation was the only theory of origins that should be taught in the Tennessee public schools.

How times change! We can now quote the words of the evolutionist, Darrow, against contemporary evolutionists who think that evolution is the only theory of origins we should teach in the public schools. The shoe is now on the other foot. The bigotry once attributed to creationists now rests squarely on the shoulders of evolutionists.

History is full of paradoxes but surely one of the strangest of all time is this — that creationists in the late twentieth century should be giving instructions to the evolutionists on the proper operation of the scientific method. Yet this is exactly what has developed in the last two decades in the United States. In their zeal to keep creation out of the curriculum, evolutionists have done violence to the best principles of science and creationists are pleading for a return to those principles.

To see this paradox in its fulness, we need to have a brief discussion of the scientific method.

THE ANATOMY OF A THEORY

This book is about theories of origins and we therefore need to know what we mean by the term "theory." The word comes from the Greek verb, *theoreo*, which means "I behold" or "I perceive." A theory, therefore, is something conceptual, something I conceive or comprehend, something I behold in a conceptual sense but not in a direct sense. You don't see a theory in the same sense you see the data it explains. A theory is a concept that interrelates and unifies the facts of observation. It is an understanding, a comprehension that imposes order and meaning on a body of data.

This analogy may help: the facts of observation are like the pieces of a jig-saw puzzle, while the theory is the picture that emerges when you get all the pieces together. Even before you finish the puzzle the picture helps you get the pieces together. The puzzle would take a very long time to work if you fitted the pieces together by just looking at the shaped pieces instead of visualizing the final picture.

To vary the metaphor, devising a good theory is like throwing a magnet into a pile of metal scraps. The pieces of metal suddenly turn toward the magnet and arrange themselves into a pattern. In the same manner a viable theory causes the facts of experience to "turn toward" it and arrange themselves in a special way, into a paradigm that satisfies the intellect.

A good theory accomplishes three things:

(1) *It explains the facts of observation.* It throws the observed data into a configuration that is clear and that makes sense to the reason.

(2) *It points to new areas of research.* It opens up new avenues of observation. If it is a good theory, the new data it uncovers will tend to support the original theory.

(3) *It allows you to make predictions of the future that will check with experience by testing.* The planet Neptune, for example, was discovered, not by random observation, but by a deliberate search. Its existence had been predicted as a necessary implication of the theory of gravitation.

At this point we logically introduce the major objection of the evolutionist to the consideration of creation — that it is not a scientific theory, but rather a religious belief. This is a faulty dilemma; the objection is obviously based on a narrow definition of the terms "scientific" and "religious." So far, it is difficult to see anything about a theory of origins that would rule out a creative deity. If you reply that God is invisible and his existence therefore can't function as a theory you will also eliminate many things that were first postulated but not seen — atoms, germs, radium, Neptune. Carlo Lastrucci writes:

> A theory ... is a generalized, synthetic explanatory statement of the "cause" of a phenomenon or of the interrelation between classes of phenomena. As such, it often employs abstractions having no apparent empirical qualities (e.g. "force," "symbiosis," "intelligence," "social mobility"). Its function is to serve as the unifying explanation for an unlimited series of possible deducible hypotheses; just as it may "explain" or systematically account for — the relationship among laws.[1]

If, as Lastrucci says, intelligence can function as a scientific theory, what would be wrong with a creative intelligence (= God) functioning as a theory? In 1950 British astronomer Fred Hoyle proposed a strange cosmological theory called

"Continuous Creation," also known as the "Steady-State Theory." Hoyle defended it by saying:

> This may seem a strange idea and I agree that it is, but in science it does not matter how strange an idea might seem so long as it works — that is to say, so long as the idea can be expressed in a precise form and so long as its consequences are found to be in agreement with observation.[2]

It would seem, then, that only an unfair definition of the kind of being in question could eliminate God as a scientific theory. To reject God as strange and non-empirical is not enough. Hence, Norman D. Newell thrashes at a strawman when he complains that "at a juncture when science and technology have split the atom, cracked the genetic code, and put men on the moon, the current revival of pre-Darwinian theory has an eerie, dreamlike quality."[3] The adjectives, "pre-Darwinian," "eerie," and "dreamlike" are totally irrelevant to this discussion, mere emotive terms designed to prejudice the case against creation before the discussion can even get started.

One doesn't have to read far in the current creation-evolution controversy to discover that the words "scientific" and "religious" are used very loosely in our culture. To object that creation is religion and therefore not science is to gloss over a complicated philosophical problem. This objection assumes that the general public instantly knows precisely what these terms mean and that they know the distinction between them. As a matter of fact, most people use these terms so loosely that no intelligent discussion on the topic can occur until they are defined.

To expedite the discussion of this issue on the popular level, therefore, I suggest that we employ two phrases, "strict science" and "loose science."

(1) *By strict science, I mean the classical, empirical method rigorously applied, so rigorously applied that one could use the term "knowledge" of the results.* Strict science desires to have

direct empirical contact by the observer of an entity, process or event. Strict science desires to have experimentation and repetition of the event or process under investigation. When a theory reaches the status of a law it implies that the result is so certain that experimenters around the world can work the same experiment and get the same results.

(2) *By loose science, I mean a less rigorous, less conclusive use of the empirical method.* You use loose science when you suggest a hypothesis to correlate a body of data, when you argue from circumstantial evidence, when you build up a case on inferential material. One can see science in this sense operating in a court of law. A good lawyer can't always produce the event he is trying to prove (e.g. "Jones killed Brown"), but he can show that all the evidence points to that conclusion. He builds up a cogent scenario; he makes the jury "see" the event *through* the data. He argues: "Jones must have killed Brown because that is the only possible way to explain all this incriminating evidence." If the lawyer does his job well, the jury will have no regrets when they pronounce Jones guilty.

In a word, strict science would refer roughly to *observation*, while loose science would refer more to *inference*. It is true that observation and inference work together in the historical scientific method but this distinction is still real and useful, especially when we deal with questions that can't be settled by the strict scientific method.

Origins is such a question! This means not only the origins of animal-vegetable forms but the origins of life itself and even the origins of the entire universe. A moment's reflection will reveal to the careful thinker that origins can never be treated like an exact science. Whatever happened, creation or evolution, it happened a long, long time ago. No human was there to observe it — no eyewitness, no scientist, no newspaper reporter, no photographer. We can't go back in a time machine to check any theory of origins. We can't experiment today to settle what happened long ago, although a lot of people make the mistake of thinking we can.

What all this means is that origins will forever — yes *forever* — be a question of loose science. There is no possible way that strict science can handle it. We are locked up, doomed to argue from inference, not direct observation. Origins, then, is a question akin to history, because you can never get at an event directly; you can only approach the event indirectly, through inferential data.

Now, all this may sound trite, but a lot of people do not seem to recognize this distinction. Many evolutionists have a bad habit of talking as if evolution were as clearly established as the Law of Gravity or Boyle's Law of Gases. Failure to grasp the distinction between observation and inference makes many people think that if science could create life in the laboratory today that would settle how life originated long ago. This is simply not true. Creating life today would not at all settle how life first began. The one is contemporary science; the other is past history. You don't necessarily settle past history by contemporary experiment. The most you might prove is what might have happened in the past, not what really did happen. For example, with modern tools we can duplicate exactly the huge stone monoliths of Stonehenge and Easter Island, but that would not prove anything about how those primitive people first produced them.

But evolutionists don't like to be pushed out of the temple of strict science. They don't want their discipline classified with history and the social sciences. So they fight back — they strain to make the evidence prove evolution absolutely and conclusively, which it can never do. They thereby commit the logical fallacy of *Special Pleading*.[4] You commit this fallacy when you dramatize the material that favors your position and ignore or belittle the material that weighs against your position. A good illustration of special pleading was the landlord who proved to the building inspector that he was providing enough heat for an apartment he owned — but he had hung the thermometer on the radiator instead of on the wall.

EVIDENCE FOR EVOLUTION

If we now look at the various lines of evidence for the theory of evolution we will find the proof is not at all conclusive. We will find that the model of creation can explain the data just as well as evolution, perhaps better in some cases.

(1) *Comparative Anatomy* supposedly proves that similar animals have a common ancestry. You can easily see an analogy between nails and hooves, hands and claws, fish scales and bird feathers. There is certainly a striking structural similarity between a bat's wing, a man's arm, and a whale's flipper. But then, does structural similarity demand genetic relationship? How do you know for sure that a Creator-Designer would not also come up with similar structures? Since the laws of motion, aerodynamics, and hydrodynamics are the same all over the earth, and perhaps the cosmos, would it not be reasonable to suppose that a Designer would make wings that resemble arms, scales that resemble feathers, arms that resemble flippers, and nails that resemble hooves? Thus comparative anatomy proves nothing in particular since the same data can be fitted to either model.[5]

(2) *Comparative Embryology* seems to support evolution. The embryos of many animals, including man, do resemble each other at early stages, prompting evolutionists to claim that man in the course of his embryonic development repeats the evolutionary history of the phylum to which he belongs. However, this proof is seldom used anymore since it is so shaky and fanciful; it leads to incredible complexities and contradictions when you try to establish exact parallels between various organs of different classes of animals.

(3) *Vestigial Organs* such as the appendix, the caecum, and the tonsils are often cited as proof of evolution. Such organs, it is argued, were once functional but lost their usefulness and gradually deteriorated. But this evidence, too, is very weak, since the creation model can easily incorporate a concept of "decaying organs" into its network of assumptions. Furthermore, it is quite possible that many organs have a function that we haven't yet discovered. Doctors are by no means universally agreed that the appendix is useless; furthermore, cells of the tonsils produce helpful antibodies.

(4) *Artificial Breeding* seems to provide proof for evolution. For example, Luther Burbank developed the Idaho potato by careful selective breeding and so people argue that nature might have produced over long ages what man has done recently with deliberate foresight. As long as they keep the word "might" in that assertion everything will be fine, but, as noted earlier, evolutionists have an almost uncontrollable temptation to assert that artificial breeding is positive proof for evolution. This is wrong.

We often call artificial breeding *micro-evolution,* which simply refers to small changes in plant and animal forms that can be observed by contemporary science. Micro-evolution is an observed fact that creationists don't contest; it happens every time we develop a new rose or breed a new variety of dog. Perhaps we would do better to refer to this process as *variation, mutation,* or *speciation.* This kind of evolution is not necessarily naturalistic. It does not rule out the possibility of creation. It has no compelling metaphysical implications.

But micro-evolution does not prove *macro-evolution,* the kind of radical change in life forms asserted by the General Theory of Evolution. Evolutionists sometimes refer to this General Theory as a journey all the way from "matter to man," or "molecules to man," or "amoeba to man," or "particles to people." This view of life is necessarily naturalistic, non-theistic, materialistic, mechanistic, and deterministic. But Macro-evolution is still only a theory; it can't be proved as strict science.[6]

Ever since Darwin, General Evolution or Macro-evolution has suffered from the lack of a mechanism. If this type of evolution were true you would have more beneficial mutations, since this is the alleged mechanism that drives life upward in its eternal complexification. All geneticists, however, such as Goldschmidt, Winchester, Glass, and Mueller, agree that 99% of all mutations are either neutral or lethal. Richard Goldschmidt reminds us that, "It is good to keep in mind . . . that nobody has ever succeeded in producing a new species, not to mention the higher categories, by selection of micro-mutations."[7]

(5) *The fossil record* is the last refuge for the evolutionist, and, incidentally, the best source of evidence for the theory. Most evolutionists admit that if you can't prove evolution there, all the other arguments would be inconclusive. The fossil record shows that various animal forms once existed that are now extinct, and it seems to suggest that in certain cases there has been a gradual development of anatomical structures through successive stages from simple to complex.

But once again the evolutionist is too eager to reach his conclusion. He must confess to certain deficiences in the fossil record. As a source of decisive evidence it is very incomplete. Our existing fossils aren't a true random sample of all animal types that lived in the past; most of them are over-represented by organisms from shallow seas, swampy areas, river mouths, and bogs. J.H.Hamon compares the entire paleontological record to a 400 page novel in which we have only pages 13, 38, 170, 340, and 400.[8] This would be roughly analogous to the District Attorney standing up in court and saying, "Ladies and gentlemen of the jury, most of the evidence for the defendant's guilt comes from his house, but unfortunately his house just burned down. We still feel, however, that he is guilty!"

The fossil record contains some evidence that actually weighs against evolution. First, there is the question of those famous "missing links." There are almost no transitional forms between great groups of animals. These missing links are also missing in animals that are alive today; in fact, the gaps in the fossil record correspond closely to the gaps we have in animal and plant groups today. For instance, nearly all new categories above the level of family (i.e., order, class, phylum) appear in the fossil record suddenly, and are not led up to by any gradual, completely continuous, transitional forms. There is a salient gap from protozoa to metazoa, from fish to amphibians, from amphibians to reptiles, from reptiles to birds and mammals and from invertebrates to vertebrates.[9] Ever since Darwin evolutionists have been searching for these missing links; they have become a kind of Holy Grail for the religious evolutionist. But over a century has passed and they are still missing and the evolutionist still has great difficulty explaining why they are missing.

Second, there was a sudden explosion of complex forms in the oldest rock strata, called the Cambrian. More than five thousand species representing almost all the major phyla of animals appear in these early rocks with no apparent antecedents. In the Cambrian layers we find lamp shells, moss animals, worms, trilobites, and shrimp. These creatures had complex organs: intestines, stomachs, bristles, spines, appendages, eyes, feelers, gills, and mouthpieces. The question needs answering: *Where are the antecedents of these Cambrian animals?* Doesn't the appearance of something without antecedents suggest the distinct possibility of creation?

Obviously, then, the fossil record is not an open-and-shut case for evolution.[10] The missing links and the Cambrian fossils clearly suggest creation rather than evolution. They certainly make creation one of the clear possibilities for origins.

We see, therefore, that the various "proofs for evolution" fall short of placing the theory in the realm of strict science. They place it definitely in the realm of loose science, where it must learn to co-exist with creation or any other model that might be in the same category. If evolutionists resist this classification it just shows that they have a philosophical-religious prejudice, which is ironic in view of the fact that they make this same charge against the creationists.

THE ERROR OF SCIENTISM

As noted before, evolutionists are fond of affirming that evolution is the only real scientific view of origins, while creation is religious and not worthy of consideration. We have tried to show, however, that this distinction is indefensible and is based on a naturalistic prejudice. But why is such a view prevalent in our time?

We live in the so-called "Age of Science" and it is understandable that the error of *Scientism* should be one of the most egregious mistakes of the *Zeitgeist* ("spirit of the times"). Scientism is an uncritical worship of the empirical scientific method, an excessive veneration of laboratory technique. To a person who commits this error, "science" is a sacred word and the phrase, "science has proved," has the force of a papal bull. To such people science has become a religion.

Thinkers who commit this error urge us to study the concrete, empirical, tangible world. This Great Commandment has its flip side; avoid the unseen, spiritual, metaphysical world, because that world really doesn't exist. But this advice will lead to the neglect of much of reality. Reality in its fullest sense is extremely complex. It contains intuitions of value and significance; it contains love, beauty, mystical ecstasy, and intimations of divinity. Science doesn't possess intellectual instruments with which to deal with all these subjective, non-empirical aspects of reality. Consequently, it ignores them and concentrates its attention to those traits of the world that it can handle by means of arithmetic, geometry, and the various branches of higher mathematics.

If you emphasize only the external, physical aspects of reality, you will, as Christ predicted, remain ignorant of some deeper dimensions of existence. Jesus accused the scholars of his own day of being scientifically precocious but spiritually retarded. "When you see a cloud rising in the west, you say at once, 'A shower is coming'; and so it happens. And when you see the south wind blowing, you say, 'There will be scorching heat'; and it happens. You hypocrites! You know how to interpret the appearance of earth and sky; but why do you not know how to interpret the present time?" (Luke 12:54-56, RSV).

We in the modern world have this same paradox: scientific advancement alongside spiritual poverty. This stems partly from the astounding success of the scientific method in our century. People look at computers, airplanes, space ships, and laser beams and exclaim that "science produces certainty," not realizing that this is true only if you grant the colossal reductionism that goes on in the scientific method.

Ask yourself this question: why do scientists so easily reject religion, non-empirical data, subjective factors, emotions, feelings, and values from their investigations? These things seem very real to most people — why, then, are they systematically ignored? The answer seems to be: because it is convenient! Since the scientific method won't allow you to deal with the immense complexity of total reality, the scientist *selects* from the whole of experience only those elements that can be weighed, measured, numbered, or which lend themselves to mathematical treatment. By using this technique of simplification and abstraction the scientist has succeeded to an astonishing degree in understanding and controlling the physical environment. This success can be intoxicating and thus many scientists jumped to the conclusion that their useful abstraction from reality was the whole of reality itself.

This is an old logical fallacy; we call it reductionism. You commit the *Reductive Fallacy* when you select a portion of a complex entity and say that the whole is merely that portion. Sir Arthur Eddington once used a fine analogy to illustrate this mistake. He told of a fisherman who concluded from his fishing experiments with a certain net that "no creature of the sea is less than two inches long." Now this law disturbed many of his colleagues and they demurred, pointing out that many sea creatures are under two inches and they just slipped through the two inch holes in the net. But the ichthyologist was unmoved. "What my net can't catch ain't fish," he pontificated, and then scornfully accused his critics of having pre-scientific, medieval, metaphysical prejudices.

Once you recognize the reductive thrust in the scientific method, it doesn't surprise you that science has a strong tendency toward materialism. As R.C.Collingwood observed:

> Materialism is the truth about any object, just in so far as the object is reducible to terms of pure mathematics; and no object is reducible except by consciously or unconsciously shutting our eyes to everything that differentiates it from everything else. This conscious or unconscious act of abstraction is the very being of the scientific consciousness, and it is therefore no matter for pained surprise when science shows a bias towards determinism, behaviourism, and materialism generally.[11]

Happily, many recent thinkers have recognized and denounced this reductive strain in the philosophy of scientific materialism. Abraham Maslow spoke for this group when he said, "The classical philosophy of science as morally neutral, value neutral, is not only wrong, but is extremely dangerous.[12] Just how dangerous can be seen by looking at the history of Germany during the Third Reich (1933-45). Nazi thinkers carried Darwinian reductionism to its logical conclusion and finally attempted *genocide* — the elimination of an entire race. Alan

Bullock was correct in saying that the core of Nazi ideology was a "crude Social Darwinism."[13]

SOCIAL DARWINISM

Jesus Christ told us that we would know an idea by its fruits. It was during the Third Reich that the evil fruit of Social Darwinism began to fall on the ground and people naturally began to re-examine some of the assumptions of evolution. The Nazis committed a fallacy in their racial views, a logical error that is subtle and difficult to detect. We need to explain it carefully. It is called the *Genetic Fallacy,* which is a special form of the Reductive Fallacy. You commit it when you claim that something is "merely" or "nothing but" its *genesis,* its origins. A common form of this mistake is to belittle something just because of its humble beginnings. Whoever makes this error overlooks the patent fact of human experience that many great and wonderful things in life began in very humble ways. For example, a man starts out as a single fertilized ovum, but it would be ridiculous for you to walk up to a fifty-year-old man and say, "You're nothing but a fertilized ovum walking around!"[14]

Social Darwinians insist that since man *began* as an animal he isn't much more than one now, just a very complex animal. They fail to see that with man you reach a new rung on the ladder of life, a psycho-social dimension that separates man from the animals by a great gulf, a gulf so wide that we really shouldn't refer to man as an animal at all. As Friedrich von Huegel argued:

> In reality, the very skin and flesh and bones of my hand or foot are not simply animal; the have been penetrated and modified, through and through, by the neural, psychological, and (more and more subtly and centrally) by the imaginative, mental, volitional, emotional life of a being precisely human.[15]

Social Darwinism throws grave doubt on the competency of two major human faculties: morality and reason. First look at morality. Evolutionists belittle morality and say it "just evolved" from animal instinct, yet no evolutionist has ever given a satisfactory explanation of how a social instinct, which some animals have, developed into a social conscience, which man alone possesses. Animal instincts are biologically inherited patterns of behavior; they are carried out automatically without conscious purpose. Human morality is something very different. You don't inherit an ethical code through biological mechanisms; there is no gene for morality. As Thomas Paine was fond of saying, "Virtue is not hereditary."

The dilemma of Darwinism is even more painful when we look at reason. Put simply: *Darwinism destroys reason!* Most evolutionists value reason but they really believe that the human intellect developed from the physical brain of the primates. The mind once didn't exist and then supposedly evolved under the stimulus of struggle. Yet despite this humble origin, reason is still trustworthy! If not, what was it that constructed the theory of evolution and defended it for over a century? Was it not reason?

But ask yourself: if the mind, like all else in nature, is still evolving, how can we be sure that its present structure and operation guarantee any truth? For example, did the Law of Contradiction, the most basic principle of thought, evolve like the rest of the physical body? I can't conceive of a half-formed Law of Contradiction. How could it possibly function in a half-formed state? Would it detect semi-contradictions? What in the world is a semi-contradiction? Furthermore, how can we be sure that there is not some new mental law, now struggling to be born, a law that will enable us to get closer to the truth about reality? Would this new law confirm, or contradict, evolution? Even Darwin, who wasn't much of a philosopher, dimly perceived the problem here:

With me, the horrid doubt always arises whether the convictions of
man's mind, which has been developed from the minds of the lower
animals, are of any value or at all trustworthy. Would anyone trust in
the convictions of a monkey's mind, if there are any convictions in
such a mind?[16]

Mortimer Adler put his finger on this very inconsistency in the
thinking of a central thinker of our time, Sigmund Freud.[17]
Freud claimed that man had the same kind of instinctual drives
as the other animals, yet man can do some unusual things to
his drives: he can *divert, postpone, subdue,* and *frustrate* them.
No other animal, says Freud, can so successfully master its
instinctual urges. In Freudian terminology, no other animal has
both civilization and its discontents.

But Freud never dealt with the crucial question clearly implied
by his own analysis: Where did reason come from? If reason
emerged from the instincts, where did it get its ability to control the instincts? Can one instinct control all the others? How?
How does reason divert, postpone, subdue, and frustrate our
drives? What strange new power enables it to master our pre-
rational urges? The power and autonomy that Freud ascribed
to reason seem possible only on the assumption that man is
radically different from the other animals. Freud denied this
assumption, but it is a key doctrine in the Christian worldview.

The conclusion seems clear. Christianity makes more sense of
man than naturalistic evolution. It explains his special features
like morality and reason better than scientific materialism. If
the evolutionary reading of man is true, then he is a profound
mystery. As G.K.Chesterton said, "We would just say that one
of the animals went off its head!" Is it not a pity that the superior hypothesis can't be taught in the public schools of the
United States?

NOTES

1. *The Scientific Approach: Basic Principles of the Scientific Method* (Cambridge, Mass.: Schenkmann Pub. Co., 1963), p. 15.

2. See Chapter 6, originally entitled "The Expanding Universe," of Hoyle's book, *The Nature of the Universe* (New York: Harper, 1950), p.124.

3. "Evolution Under Attack," *Natural History* (April, 1974), p.37.

4. See Chapter 17 of my book, *Don't You Believe It! Poking Holes in Faulty Logic* (Chicago: Moody Press, 1982), pp. 83-87.

5. This conclusion is admitted by a leading European evolutionist, Sir Gavin de Beer in his *Homology, An Unsolved Problem* (London: Oxford Univ. Press, 1971), p.15.

6. This is admitted by nearly all evolutionists; e.g., see Theodosius Dobzhansky, "On Methods of Evolutionary Biology and Anthropology," *American Scientist*, Vol..45 (December, 1957), p.388.

7. *Theoretical Genetics* (Berkeley: Univ. of California Press, 1955), p. 153.

8. Cited in John W. Klotz, "Creationist Viewpoints," *A Symposium On Creation* (Grand Rapids, Michigan: Baker Book House, 1968), p. 50.

9. This is admitted by nearly all evolutionists; e.g., see George G. Simpson, *The Major Features of Evolution* (New York: Columbia Univ. Press, 1953), p. 360.

10. For a good summary of the weaknesses of this line of proof, see Steven A. Austin, "Ten Misconceptions about the Geologic Column," Article #137 of *Impact* (November, 1984), published by the Institute of Creation Research, El Cajon, California.

11. *Speculum Mentis*, p.. 168; cited in Alan Richardson's *Christian Apologetics* (New York: Harper and Row, 1947). p.29.

12. *American Psychologist*, 24:274.

13. *Hitler: A Study in Tyranny* (New York: Bantam Books, 1964), especially pp. 345-46.

14. See Chapter 4 of my book, *Don't You Believe It!*, pp. 29-33.

15. *The German Soul* (London:, 1915), p.65.

16. See the letter in Francis Darwin, ed., *Life and Letters of Charles Darwin* (1903; reprint ed., New York: Johnson Reprint, 1971), 1:285. For a good statement of the same point see C.S.Lewis, *Miracles* (New York: Macmillan, 1947), pp. 32, 109.

17. *The Difference of Man and the Difference it Makes* (New York: Holt, Rinehart, and Winston, 1967), pp. 276ff. Freud's position is stated in his *Civilization and Its Discontents*, trans. J. Riviere (New York: Jonathan Cape and Harrison Smith, 1930). For a good presentation of the difficulty Marxism has in explaining man's unique features see John F. Crosby,

Science and Evolution

3

GEOLOGY AND PALEONTOLOGY

CHARLES FELIX

*T*here exists an intricate mixture of aspects of geology and biology, that must be considered if the Christian is to be comfortable with his religious beliefs in today's scientific environment. Seemingly, evolution is a problem in the biological area, but any appraisal of organic evolution and its impact upon a Christian's faith must by necessity require some insight into geological principles, fossil occurrences, the ages of the earth's rocks, and even the contributions of investigators such as Charles Darwin. The issues are not simple, nor are easy answers available.

UNIFORMITARIANISM — CATASTROPHISM

Probably somewhat confusing to the Christian are the formidable concepts of *Uniformitarianism* and *Catastrophism* and one may justifiably question what these have to do with a more complete understanding of the Bible and of God. *Uniformitarianism is the great underlying principle of modern geology!* The Scottish geologist, James Hutton, is usually credited with developing the principle about 1785, but the English geologist

Charles Lyell is generally considered as the most responsible person for the concept's refinement about 1830. Simply stated, it suggests that all geologic features of the past were produced by processes which are still functioning today. The inference is that it has always rained as at present, earth erosion has occurred at the same pace, and rocks have accumulated in the same manner. The principle has popularly been referred to as "The Present is the Key to the Past," and according to it the natural processes we see at work on earth today are supposedly sufficient to account for all past events.

By necessity such a concept as Uniformitarianism would require vast amounts of time to account for all the geological events and structures of the present day earth. This would, of course, include the distribution of fossils, so important in any explanation of organic evolution. Early opposition to Uniformitarianism existed, largely based upon religious grounds, because it necessitated an earth of great antiquity, and seemingly in disagreement with the Genesis record.

In contrast, the concept of *Catastrophism* gained popularity in that it provided an accounting for geological events more in agreement with Biblical creation accounts. This concept was advanced by the French paleontologist, George Cuvier, who theorized that the earth had periodically been the scene of great catastrophes, the Genesis flood being the most recent of these. Therefore, Catastrophism could conceivably produce physical evidence of the Flood, as well as provide much shorter time-spans for development than would be required for Uniformitarianism.

Uniformitarianism endures, partly because it seems reasonable and the principle is considered basic to other fields of study, but it also persists because *this is the only way to arrive at the enormous time-frame required for placement of slow evolutionary processes.* It is probably correct to state that evolution depends upon the unqualified acceptance of Uniformitarianism! Also, it should be noted that historical geology deals with events that are past, and therefore they are not reproducible. Uniformitarianism, therefore, is only a reasonable assumption; nothing more, nothing less. The geologist of today is also burdened with *the geological timetable,* a necessity for demonstrating evolutionary development, but a concept which is based entirely upon uniformitarian processes.

If geologic events of catastrophic proportions could be demonstrated to have occurred in the past, then perhaps doubt could be cast upon the validity of Uniformitarianism and its organic evolution association. The uniformitarians have regarded the world as changing gradually and slowly, thus allowing enough time for adaptation to achieve the evolutionary goal of progress. Evidence now suggests that environmental conditions have changed suddenly and drastically, with mass extinctions resulting. This has been aptly phrased as "the survival of the luckiest," rather than Darwin's "Survival of the Fittest."[1] It is popular today to note that catastrophes not only occurred in the past, but are still taking place. A somewhat time-worn example of this is usually that of the awesome volcanic eruption of Krakatoa in the East Indies in 1883. The explosion was heard 3,000 miles away, and ash and debris fell over a 300,000 square mile area, while great tidal waves destroyed hundreds of towns, and some 40,000 persons died on the islands of Java and Sumatra. There is also evidence that giant extra-terrestrial masses have cataclysmically impacted the earth, and undeniable proof exists of enormous sheets of ice having once covered large parts of the earth.

However, despite the enormity of these events and the damage they wrought, they were still relatively local and actually minor. It is likely that Krakatoa went unnoticed by the majority of the world, and in all probability life went on unaffected in the southern hemisphere when most of the northern hemisphere lay in the grip of the frozen Ice Age. To give validity to catastrophism and to theorize on the occurrence of an event of the magnitude of the biblical flood, the impact would have to be universal in scope. If such a happening could be demonstrated, then the Genesis Flood could be considered to be a reality and the geological timetable and its attendant organic evolution progression would be rendered suspect.

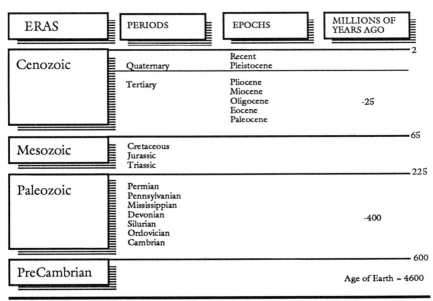

Figure 1. Geologic Timetable. Showing relative position of rocks of the Earth.

THE GEOLOGIC TIMETABLE

The above device (Figure 1) may well be referred to as the "cornerstone" of geology. It portrays the rock units of the earth in an orderly arrangement from the oldest to the youngest, with the included fossils preserved in an orderly evolutionary sequence. It is a type of calendar for the geologist and provides a common basis of communication among scientists. Perhaps more than any other principle of geology, it is portrayed as the absolute proof for the earth's antiquity and for the evolutionary development of life.

Basically this scheme seems reasonable enough, and it is true that over large areas of the earth, rock units exist that are similar in character and have comparable fossils. Economic use is made of the time-scale. However, this time-scale has problems and inconsistencies. The reader should realize that this orderly sequence of rock units does not exist at any one specific location on earth. So this "idealized chart" (Figure 1) is actually no more than a piecemeal arrangement, the portions of which are located at widely diverse geographical points. The much publicized time-table does not portray any orderly progression of life, and its most accurate contribution is only to demonstrate a contemporaneous deposition of sediments in many places on the earth. It would make little difference whether fossil remains were deposited ten years or ten million years ago or whether they were deposited within a time of ten hours or ten thousand years. In settling out in water, natural physical laws would require that the fossils, in fact all sedimentary particles, would assume certain unique groupings on the basis of difference in size, shape, and weight.

The time-scale has its serious problems and inconsistencies. It is fraught with instances of rock beds out of their supposed proper sequences; formations completely missing; and misplaced fossils. In many instances there are explanations for many of these anomalies, but the time-scale has had to assume a basically defensive posture. Paradoxically, geology argues in a circle where the time-scale is concerned. Instances exist of fossil flora and fauna dated by the rocks containing them; while on the other hand some rocks are dated on the basis of their included fossils. This is a common, though unscientific, practice.

The "idealized" sequence of rocks commonly presented is based upon sedimentary rocks, representing rocks usually deposited by water and including fragments of pre-existing rocks. The extreme dates assigned these units are based upon igneous rocks, composed of volcanic (or at least extreme heat) origins. Each unit is also characterized by a unit, existing somewhere on the earth's surface, and serving as a "type" or reference standard. For instance, the Silurian type area is in South Wales, the Devonian near Devonshire, England, the Permian close to the Russian village of Perm in the Ural mountains, and the Mississippian from the Mississippi River Basin of the U.S.A.

It must be realized that in using the geologic time-table, one utilizes a structure in which the periods are not natural time units but are rather artificial subdivisions that must be arbitrarily separated out from each other. The table survives today only as a set of arbitrarily and pragmatically defined rock units tied to the supposed evolution of living species, rather than to actual historical and physical events.

PALEONTOLOGY

Properly speaking, this field is also a phase of geology, although so specialized at times as to appear completely removed from general earth science. Paleontology deals with fossils, the preserved remains of plant and animal life of the past. Some 250 years ago one of geology's basic premises, *The Principle of Faunal Succession*, was formulated. It basically stated that fossils occur in the geologic record in a definite and determinable order and that divisions of geologic time may therefore be identified by the included fossils.

Today, however, it is almost unanimously agreed among geologists that the strongest, and even indisputable, evidence for organic evolution comes from paleontology. The sedimentary rocks of the earth often contain abundant plant and animal fossils, and these are sufficiently diagnostic as to allow similar rocks to be identified, though separated over considerable distances. Fossils also appear to change significantly from older to younger rocks, thus providing the basis for changes interpreted as evolution. However, one must remain cognizant of the fact that we can only theorize that these diagnostic patterns exist, and we must remember that a complete section of such rocks does not exist anywhere on earth. In essence, what we have is a skillfully contrived and orderly arranged succession of fossils, since the paleontologist can place them where they best fit into a theoretical evolutionary scheme. The disciple of paleontology has been characterized by one distinguished paleontologist as being comparable to dealing with a 10,000 piece jigsaw puzzle for which you have only 15 pieces.[2]

It is quite true that various rocks can be identified by their included fossils, and economic utility results from the ability to correlate rock strata which are separated by considerable distances. However, this process does not necessarily denote organic evolution but only implies a contemporaneous deposition of the sediments forming the evolutionary change that holds for "broad gaps." This is the "punctuation evolution" of S.M. Stanley and the "punctuated equilibrium" of S.J. Gould, in which species are claimed to have evolved during some periods, resulting in a sudden "emergence" from parental stocks, and then to have remained stable for longs periods of time. However, if "punctuated equilibrium" or "evolution" operates in a manner to leave no fossil evidence, then in terms of paleontology the theory rests largely upon negative evidence, which is an unacceptable concept under Darwinism.

One of the most significant examples of a "missing link" has long been *Archeopteryx*, considered to be the earliest known bird but with reptilian characteristics and thus serving as the transitional form between cold-blooded reptiles and warm-blooded birds. However, it has been noted that there are birds extant today which possess the primitive features of *Archeopteryx, such as claws on the wings and elongated caudal vertebrae.*

In 1977 Brigham Young University scientists discovered fossil remains of an unequivocal modern bird in rocks of the same period as Archeopteryx, which supposedly predated true birds by 60 million years. One of the better known instances of embarassment to the evolutionist has also been the case of the coelacanth, *Latimeria chalumnae.* This animal had long been recognized as having thrived in the Devonian seas and was regarded as an important representative of the so-called armored fish, Crossopterygii. It was considered to have been a key evolutionary link to the land vertebrates, and it has been popular to portray it as being the point when life left its aquatic habitat and walked on land, eventually giving rise to the amphibians. Textbooks were liberally cluttered with theorizing about this key "missing link," but the world of paleontology was astounded in December, 1937, when a fishing trawler netted a coelacanth near the South African port of East London. Since that time scores of these primitive fish have been captured, most from the Madagascar and Comores waters of Africa. One specimen taken in 1954 survived over 30 hours.

THE BIBLE FLOOD

Perhaps no greater area of disagreement exists between the Christian and the scientific community than the subject of the Genesis Flood. At one time, in the not too distant past, such a universal flood was considered to be the explanation for most geological events. However, most geologists and paleontologists of today present a substantially united front against the occurrence of such an event. Perhaps no event could better substantiate the accuracy of the Bible than would definite proof that the entire world was once inundated by water. Again and again the debate regarding the accuracy of the scriptures returns to the flood story, and Christians seek tirelessly for its evidence, and they examine and conjecture concerning the evidence from Mount Ararat. Indeed, catastrophic events have occurred that provide encouragement to believers, and various investigators sympathetic to the Christian view have tied the catastrophic events of the great frozen mammal deposits of Siberia, the Ice Age, and Plate Tectonics to this flood. Plate Tectonics theorizes that the earth's crust is a brittle shell consisting of several large land masses (plates) that move on an underlying semi-molten, plastic layer. The result is a constantly changing surface and displacement of the continents themselves.

The geologist has a valid role in this, for if a universal flood did occur, it was also a geological event in that it would have necessarily disrupted sedimentary processes, produced intense erosion, displaced great parts of the earth, changed and obliterated the courses of rivers, and created a vast mausoleum of potential fossil entities. Mass chaos should have been the end result, but how does one account for the seemingly orderly sedimentary processes of the present day and the apparent evidence that they occurred in like fashion in the past? However, it seems reasonable that if the entire earth were once inundated, a prolonged settling out effect would have followed as the encompassing waters receded, most likely into the earth's crustal structure itself. Certainly geologic principles would have been in operation, and an orderly deposition of the earth's disturbed surface would have occurred.

In considering the Bible Flood, it is likely that inflexible opinions exist, for the supernatural exists as a permanent barrier to any compromise between the Christian and most geologists, and admittedly the Genesis Flood was a supernatural event. Among the factors unacceptable to most scientists are:

1. *Physical scientists contend that an impossible amount of rain fell.* Under the physical laws in operation today, such a source of water does not exist.

2. *God spoke directly to Noah.* Certainly, in today's materialistic society, one would find it difficult to accept such communication from the Creator.

3. *Noah was 600 years old at the time of the flood,* an unacceptable length of life today.

4. *The gathering of animals was abnormal,* for they came directly to Noah.

Now, however, there is ample evidence that geologic events of a catastrophic magnitude and involving water have occurred in the earth's past. An enormous accumulation of fossils have been unearthed recently on Nova Scotia and commented on by paleontologists as being especially unique because the sandstone matrix is packed with so many skeletal fragments as to be described as "bone hash." A catastrophic extinction is theorized for these animals, and researchers from Columbia and Harvard universities believe this catastrophism to be the result of meteorite or comet impact.[3]

THE FROZEN MAMMALS OF SIBERIA

An often ignored enigma of paleontology has been the extraordinary mammal deposits of the north polar latitudes, especially the Siberian mammoth-deposit occurrences. Their presence has long been known, but it has been somewhat difficult to separate fact from fiction. The usual explanation by geologists and paleontologists for their existence has been one based on Uniformitarianism — that they represent animals accidentally killed, probably having fallen into crevices in the ice. Difficult to explain, and largely ignored, have been the staggering numbers of the animals, the curious fact that many died in upright positions, the presence of undigested food in their mouths and stomachs, and that this food could not have grown in the icy north. These problems have been rather casually dismissed by present day geologists. The Russian scientist Tolmachoff,[4] has provided much information of the mammoths. He noted that in one 250 year period Siberian trading posts handled commercial tusks of ivory of nearly 50,000 of these giant animals.

An isolated specimen or a few individuals might well be explained by natural uniformitarian causes, but such great numbers to be found without evident decay, undisturbed by predators, with mouths filled with food, can only point to catastrophes. These great animals had their existence ended very suddenly. It is unreasonable to assume that tens of thousands of these giant beasts suddenly stumbled to their deaths over hundreds of thousands of square miles. Some of the scientific explanations for their demise tax the credulity of the Christian to a great degree as do the miracles of the Bible to an unbelieving scientist.

THE FROZEN FORESTS OF THE ARCTIC

A little known, or exploited, phenomenon as spectacular and as lacking in satisfactory explanation as the frozen animals of Siberia exists in the north polar regions of the western hemisphere. For many years this writer has engaged in geological and paleontological work in the Arctic islands of the Northwest Territories of Canada (Figure 2).

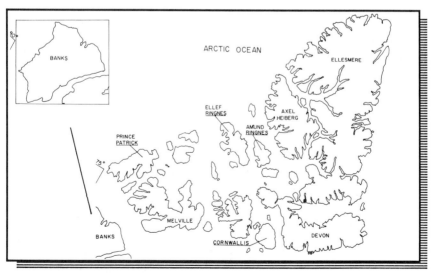

Figure 2. Map of the Artic Islands of the northwest territories of Canada.

These studies have revealed that this vast frozen wasteland was once covered by luxuriant forests similar to those in the present day temperate climates, and this flora was circumpolar in extent and it extended down into the frozen deserts of Siberia. Great forests of the past, apparently fossilized, exist across the Arctic, and I have collected their remains from Ellef Ringnes, Axel Heiberg, and Ellesmere islands. Recently the Canadian geologist, Basinger,[5] unearthed the remains of 19 distinct forest layers on Axel Heiberg island (Figure 2). The intriguing aspect of these so-called fossilized forests is that they are not fossilized but are simply dried or "mummified." The wood will burn readily, which would not be so if the material were truly fossilized. I have found these unusual plant associations abundant everywhere north of 70 degrees north latitude, where today the area is devoid of normal trees, where the long winter night begins in early November when the sun does not rise, and ends in early February with a momentary sunrise, and where the temperature falls to minus 60 degrees Fahrenheit during the dark winter months. All indications are that the great, green temperate forests perished dreadfully quickly. A cataclysmic event of universal proportions destroyed their world very quickly. No uniformitarianism involving slow fossilization occurred here, but rather the evidence is for a world in disaster. Whether or not it was the Genesis Flood is open to speculation, but certainly it was an event of the magnitude of such a flood.

DISCUSSION

Figure 3, in comparing a scientific view with a biblical one, illustrates some similarities. In both, man came into existence in a manner that appears to have been *fiat* creation in some respects, at least for the existence of life. Science generally accepts some developmental evolution accounting for man to the point of civilization, this being roughly some 6,000 to 10,000 years ago. In studying man, anthropologists and

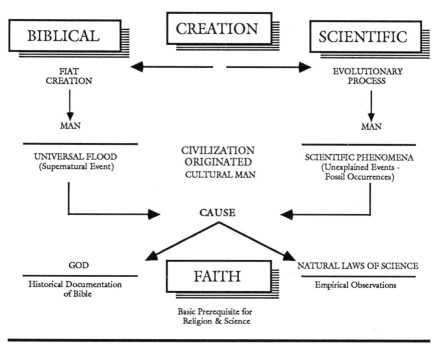

Figure 3. A comparison of a scientific creation with the biblical creation.

archaeologists again and again have encountered a blank wall historically about 6,000 years B.C., this being the time of man's appearance in the mid-east, living in civilized village cultures. Since that time, there is literal evidence that man has rapidly increased in numbers up to the vast population of today's world.

It would appear that some catastrophic event had occurred, hindering scientific efforts to interpret man's existence beyond some 10,000 years ago. Essentially this is what the Christian believes — that cultural civilization dates from a relatively recent time or after a catastrophic, universal flood inundated the earth and destroyed every vestige of man, excepting one family of eight persons. Now this makes it difficult for the Christian to convince others, for all he has is FAITH. He must rely upon faith inasmuch as the biblical flood defies logical explanation to the scientist who has a calculated, empirical approach. It was a supernatural event in which an immense amount of water was involved.

But scientifically the same thing occurred; man burst forth as a civilized entity only a few thousand years ago. There is little explanation, beyond theorizing, as to why this may have taken place after eons of evolution.

So science has the same problem as the Bible believer. Inexplicable as a universal flood might be, many events known and accepted by the scientific community rival the mystery of the Genesis flood. Many geological events defy explanation but they do exist. Among these is evidence of geological changes as manifested in Plate Tectonics, where we have indisputable evidence that great land masses, even the continents, have been torn asunder and moved thousands of miles by some mighty force. Enormous ice sheets, perhaps two miles in thickness, have covered much of the earth in time past. No effectual interpretation of the ice's origin is known. Distribution of fossil occurrences, not explainable by uniformitarianism, are numerous.

Such scientific events have occurred; the evidence is all about us. But, the scientists lack explanations of any mechanism or energy source which can account for them. Therefore, as demonstrated by Figure 3, both the scientist and the Christian are faced with the sudden appearance of civilized man only a few thousand years ago. Both are also faced with phenomena which defy logical explanations based upon literal evidence, the Christian the universal flood, and the scientist's many geological events. The Christian has always depended upon a FAITH in the Bible account to accept the credibility of the flood event. However, the scientist also has a FAITH. He has faith that the laws of nature have acted in an orderly and predictable manner and will eventually provide explanations for the numerous natural phenomena he is presently unable to explain.

It is here that the Christian stands upon the firmer foundation, for his faith is based upon a plausible mechanism — upon God. The scientist stands, as if naked, with a problem in that he has a faith but no causal mechanism to account for it. Admittedly, one cannot necessarily demonstrate that these geological phenomena are results of the Flood. However, the Flood would be regarded as a catastrophic event, and Plate Tectonics, Ice Ages, and fossils, are not explainable by Uniformitarianism. It is conceivable that a catastrophic event of the magnitude of a universal flood accounts for many of the geological enigmas.

It may justifiably be said that: *The Christian individual has more justification and stronger grounds for his acceptance of the Bible than does the scientist without the Bible, who might question his belief, for both have the convictions based upon faith, and the Christian's faith does have the support of a causal mechanism.*

In truth, it seems that most modern scientists regard the initial appearance of life and its subsequent development as accidental evolution, and they invoke accidents the way the Christian invokes God. One of the more popular science-bestsellers of recent times makes it clear that the accident is a fundamental factor in the origin of life.[6] Scientifically such a position is no more capable of proof or disproof than the miracle of special creation.

N O T E S

1. K.J. Hau, *Sedimentary Petrology and Biologic Evolution,* Journal of Sedimentary Petrologyy, Vol. 56, No.5, 1986, p.732.

2. *TIME,* August 25, 1986, p.50.

3. *LAPIDARY,* December 1986, Vol.40, No.9, p.6.

4. I.P.Tolmachoff. *The carcasses of the Mammoth and Rhinoceros found in the frozen ground of Siberia.* Transactions of the American Philosophical Society of Philadelphia, Vol. 23, 1929.

5. *TIME*, September 22, 1986, p.64. 6. Carl Sagan, Cosmos, New York: Random House, 1980.

6. Carl Sagan, *Cosmos*, New York: Random House, 1980.

4

The most beautiful and most profound emotion we can experience is the sensation of the mystical. It is the sower of all true science. He to whom this emotion is a stranger, who can no longer stand rapt in awe, is as good as dead. That deeply emotional conviction of the presence of a superior reasoning power, which is revealed in the incomprehensible universe, forms my idea of God. —*ALBERT EINSTEIN*

BIOLOGY AND EVOLUTION

JAMES R. NICHOLS

*I*n the context of this series of articles we turn to some fundamental biology topics that relate to the question of evolution. During any writing, an author makes certain assumptions about the reader. So perhaps it would only be fair if I, here at the outset, identify the assumptions I have about you as the reader. I assume (1) you are interested in the topic, (2) you do not want to be smothered with biologic detail but you do want to feel that the main points have been considered, (3) you would like to know why evolution theory is so attractive to so many scientists, and (4) you would like to have an idea of how much of the topic is fact and how much is "fancy."

Basic to our consideration of evolution as a biology topic is an understanding of "science." This topic has been dealt with elsewhere in these articles, but its importance cannot be overstated, especially as it relates to the consideration at hand. Science is based on observations. Scientific conclusions are then based on these observations. Early in the schooling of every science student, the student is introduced to "Ockham's razor," a philosophical idea, which suggests that scientific conclusions should represent the simplest explanation of the observations. (Unfortunately, what may be "simple" to one person might not be simple to another, and may even be preposterous).

Nevertheless, the idea of observations, matters which can be measured and quantified, is fundamental. This leads to two sub-points: In the first place, new observations are continually being made. If conclusions are based on obervations (which they are), this means that scientific conclusions are always tentative. A conclusion which seems quite satisfactory when based on observations made at one time may look to be very incorrect when subsequent observations are made. Every scientist accepts this and understands that new observations may either support or deny a cherished earlier conclusion. This is not to say, however, that scientists do not have anything of which they are sure. Certainly there are cases where so many consistent observations have been made that they point to a conclusion which no one doubts. For example, if you drop something, it falls to the earth; consistent observations have indicated the presence of gravity. On the other hand, some of our conclusions about the planet Saturn were altered by the spectacular photographs and measurements taken by nearby satellites a few years ago.

Second, since scientific conclusions are based on observations, that means that only those matters susceptible to observation can be dealt with scientifically. There is a fair amount of confusion on this point from at least two directions. Some would argue that science is so important that the only real things in life are, in fact, those which can be observed and measured. But this omits several aspects of life which bring richness and meaning, including morality, religion, and aesthetics. We can describe and measure some of the results of courage, but in doing so we are not really dealing with the courage itself.

We can quantify the meter and phrasing of a poem or of a symphony, but that measurement does not reflect the impact of that poem or symphony on our being. The fact is, there are many important aspects of human life which are not easily measured and are therefore outside scientific consideration.

There are others, however, who would attempt to force scientific consideration of fundamentally unobservable, unmeasurable situations. Creation and some aspects of evolution theory fit as examples here. Unless life has always existed on the earth, there must have been at least one time when life came from non-life. Today the only life we see has come from life itself; we see life as a continuous process. Since we do not today observe life coming from non-life, we find it difficult to consider the creation of life scientifically (though we may consider it emotionally or theologically). We also do not see major groups of plants and animals changing (evolving) into other groups today. Some would suggest that there is evidence that this has occurred and is continuing to occur today, only so slowly that it is imperceptible in our life span, but the fact is that we do not clearly observe this occurring today. Since science is based on observation, our "scientific" consideration of the evolution of major groups of life forms is, therefore, on shaky ground. We must understand what science can, and cannot, deal with validly.

My use of the term "major groups" above requires some clarification. For a good part of human history there have been individuals interested in grouping organisms according to similarities and differences. One of the earliest schemes for classifying organisms was proposed over two thousand years ago by Aristotle. Modern classification and organism naming owes much to Swedish naturalist Carolus Linnaeus. Avoiding unnecessary detail, modern classification basically takes the form of an outline in which the differences and similarities of organisms are used to position them in relation to each other.

The major groups like phyla and classes have significant differences from one another whereas groups on the other end of the spectrum, like genera and species, have many fewer differences and more similarities. Linnaeus suggested a scientific naming system, using Latin words, identifying the genus and species of each organism. For example, humans are referred to as Homo sapiens, with *Homo* being the genus and *sapiens* being the species. The species level represents the greatest similarity between organisms, and will be important for our later consideration.

A contemporary of Linnaeus in the nineteenth century was Gregor Mendel. Mendel, considered to be the father of modern genetics, did extensive breeding experiments with plants and concluded that during sexual reproduction, characteristics of parents were passed on to their offspring in specific and, generally predictable, ways. Mendel did not know about chromosomes or cell biology as we do today, but additions to Mendel's ideas in the early 1900's firmly established the chromosomal basis of inheritance. It is now well understood that many of the characteristics of an organism are determined by genetic information contained on chromosomes-structures found within the nucleus of every cell within a body.

Apparently unknown to Mendel, Charles Darwin and Alfred Russel Wallace were considering life in another way at about the same time. We hear most about Darwin's work in the mid-1800's, but apparently Wallace was coming to the same conclusions at about the same time. Of particular interest to Darwin and Wallace was the *variety* of organisms which existed in the world. Prompted by data gathered while he served as a naturalist on a British ship visiting South America and the Galapagos Islands, Darwin concluded that organisms had similarities and differences because they had undergone body changes (internally and externally) over time.

We might view Darwin as making two contributions to thought. His first suggestion was that organisms have an evolutionary origin. This concept was a blow against the "fixity of the species" idea, the then-prevailing notion that organisms were "fixed" with certain body forms which were unchanging. Darwin's evidence for organisms having evolved included notes on anatomic similarities and embryologic evidence (considered elsewhere herein). He attempted to group organisms by similarities and differences and said these relationships indicated common ancestors.

A second major contribution of Darwin was his proposal of natural selection as a partial explanation of how evolution might have occurred. Natural selection is a well-accepted and important biologic phenomenon today. It can be described in a series of four sub-points:

(1) *Variation exists within a species.* Organisms are not all alike. In any population of organisms there is variety. Looking at humans it is obvious we are of different heights, complexions, temperaments, tolerance of foods, etc. All cocker spaniels are not alike, even those from the same litter. Our assumption is that the same holds true for all organisms. All cockroaches or all dandelions may look alike to us, but the cockroaches apparently can distinguish one another somewhat and biochemical analysis shows differences between individuals, whether cockroaches, dandelions, or whatever.

(2) *Overpopulation of a species is a rule of nature.* Organisms tend to reproduce. Humans satisfy this point also, but it is perhaps easier for us to use non-human examples. Any parent who has allowed a child to buy just "two" mice will find many more than two soon if the originals were of the opposite sex. Any gardener knows the importance of removing the first few weed intruders in the garden.

(3) *Selection of the more "fit" organisms occurs.* Increases in population described by (2) cannot continue forever. At some

point the organisms in a population become so numerous that the competition between them for some life necessity becomes a limiting factor. There is not enough shade or light, not enough food or water, nesting places are limited —almost any life necessity can become the "weak link" in the chain which inhibits the uncontrolled population increase. (Again, I would suggest that humans are not a particularly good example to use here. We are certainly susceptible to shortages, but we are also smart enough to control our environment somewhat; for example, we can light the dark so we can be active at night, heat or cool our buildings so we do not have to live in a limited area of the earth, and have been very successful at controlling life-threatening diseases which would otherwise sweep through a population as dense as ours). When organisms begin to be so numerous that some factors are limiting, it is obvious that some of the organisms will be able to handle the problem better than others. For example, consider an animal group whose food supply consists of the leaves of certain trees. Obviously, the members of the group which are the fastest and most agile tree climbers will be at an advantage when a food shortage comes. These organisms would be described as the most "fit" for this particular environment. "Fitness" simply describes an individual organism's ability to deal with the environmental challenges present. Since variation exists, some organisms are more "fit" in a given environment than others. It is important to note that, if the environment should change, a characteristic which used to be an advantage and made an organism more "fit" may very well become a disadvantage.

(4) *Survivors have the more "fit" characteristics.* As organisms continue to reproduce in a given environment, the number of organisms with the more "fit" characteristics increases. The idea here is that, over a period of time, those organisms which can best deal with the existing environment out-reproduce those which do not deal with the environment so well. This may be only a slight out-reproducing, but over time there come to be more and more organisms with the more "fit"

characteristics (whatever they are) and fewer and fewer of the less fit. These less fit organisms do not necessarily die or stop reproducing, they just fall further and further behind in numbers. The result of this is that a population of organisms undergoes changes in characteristics over a period of time.

Darwin/Wallace's proposal of natural selection has been a major unifying idea in the modern synthesis of evolutionary theory. In the early 1900's individuals familiar with Darwin's ideas rediscovered Mendel's inheritance suggestions, and, together with increasing knowledge of cell biology, fused the ideas into modern evolutionary thought.

Evolution, a term which refers to change, is such a loaded word that it is difficult to use it without arousing preconceived biases. I would prefer to shift to a more specific idea which will allow us to deal more clearly with the modern synthesis of evolutionary theory, but will, perhaps, be on a scale that is more reasonable. The topic of consideration should be *speciation*.

The idea of a species was mentioned before, and the indication was that a species describes organisms with a great many similarities and a minimum number of differences. To be more specific, most biologists identify a species as a group of potentially interbreeding individuals. They do not have to interbreed, but, if they are in the same locale and conditions are acceptable, they can interbreed and produce fertile offspring, that is, offspring which, themselves, can successfully reproduce. There are some exceptions and problems with this definition (for example, it assumes the organisms are reproducing sexually which eliminates most microorganisms), but this definition of a species is useful.

Speciation, then, describes the *formation* of species. This would mean that one group of potentially interbreeding organisms may split into two or more such groups. In these new groups the organisms can reproduce within their own group, but not between groups. If one group of interbreeding organisms splits into two or more groups reproductively isolated from each other, speciation (the formation of species) is said to have occurred.

Perhaps I should say point blank here that many biologists believe that speciation is the simplest type of evolution and is the basis for more complex evolution. I shall return to this thought later.

Speciation is believed to occur by a particular mechanism involving several events: mutations and recombinations, natural selection, and reproductive isolation. We wish to discuss these points in some detail:

(1) *Mutations.* Chromosomes in the nucleus of each cell contain several chemical substances including deoxyribonucleic acid (DNA). The molecular structure of DNA is very precise and seems to contain a code which we understand determines the inheritable characteristics of the cell and the individual. There is a very close relationship between the actual chemical structure of DNA and the hereditary information it contains. A change in the chemical structure, even a slight one in some cases, can cause a dramatic change in the information contained. One of the best known examples is sickle-cell anemia, a condition in which the afflicted individual has unusually shaped red blood cells and subsequent significant health problems. When the DNA of an individual with sickle-cell anemia is compared with that of a "normal" individual, there is only a very slight difference in the DNA information coding for "how to make a red blood cell," but this slight change causes profound results for the individual.

Alterations in the chemical composition of the DNA are called mutations. Mutations represent actual changes in the genes, the pieces of information arranged linearly on the chromosome, like beads on a string. Although specific things speed up mutation rates (certain radiation forms and certain chemicals), mutations seem to be a fact of life, even if we could envision removing from the environment all factors which might speed up their rate.

It should be noted that most mutations are detrimental. This is reasonable. Life is very efficient; there is a great deal of balance occcurring within a cell or a body and the possibility of a random change causing an already efficient cell to become *more* efficient is not high. If I walk up to a well-tuned automobile engine, close my eyes, and twist something with a crescent wrench, I probably will not improve the performance of the engine. Everyone agrees that most mutations are negative, or at least neutral.

But by saying that, we imply that a *few* mutations are positive; they actually *do* make the organism more capable of dealing with its surroundings, more "fit." This small group of randomly occurring positive mutations serves as one of the foundations for speciation.

(2) *Recombinations.* For reasons which are not altogether clear to scientists, the actual physical arrangement of the genes on a chromosome seems to be important. Elementary genetics problems consider traits which are controlled by only one or two genes. While there are examples of that, there are also many situations where a trait of an individual is the result of a team of genes working together. For example, there is not just one gene that determines how tall we are, but a group of interacting genes. To a certain extent, the outcome is a result of what team members are present, where they are positioned, and how they interact with one another. Recombination describes any one of several events in which the genes are rearranged. Notice that these are not new or changed genes (as is mutation), but simply pre-existing genes arranged in new ways — and since arrangement is important in some cases, the expression of this gene team may be different. If we keep the same players but change their respective positions on a football team, the team will likely perform differently.

Mutations and recombinations are partners, then, each altering the genetic material in its own way. Both processes seem to occur simultaneously, and together they add a consistent variability to populations of organisms. Remember that one of the prerequisites for natural selection is that there is variation between organisms; mutations and recombinations occurring randomly are what support and maintain this variation. Mutations and recombinations cause genetic change, which is acted upon by natural selection.

(3) *Natural selection.* Speciation depends on natural selection evaluating organisms. Which organisms have the most advantageous characteristics for this particular environment? Which organisms are at a disadvantage? The changeability of the environment is a critical item here. Let us say a population of organisms exists in a locale which has fairly harsh winters. The organisms vary, as we would expect, in ability to tolerate cold. Those most cold-hardy are at an advantage and, over the long run, we would expect there to be more and more individuals with that characteristic. Suppose, however, that a major climatic change occurred resulting in milder winters and hotter summers. Now cold-hardiness is no longer an advantage, and may well be a disadvantage if it is coupled with inability to withstand heat.

In summary, then, mutations and recombinations generate genetic change which shows up as variety in organisms and then the environment determines which of those changes are positive, negative, or neutral. I should say here that, as a professional biologist for over 20 years, I have never met one biologist who doubted that mutations, recombinations, and natural selection occur. I believe we are talking about facts so far.

(4) *Reproductive isolation.* Remember, we are considering speciation — how one group of potentially interbreeding individuals splits into groups which cannot interbreed. Mutations, recombinations, and natural selection may cause organisms to have different characteristics from each other, but that

54

does not say they cannot interbreed. The topic of concern here is how some organisms might be blocked from breeding with each other. Reproductive isolation might occur in several ways and, at the risk of simplifying too much, let me identify two of the main suggestions: (A) geographic barriers, and, (B) exaggerated variability.

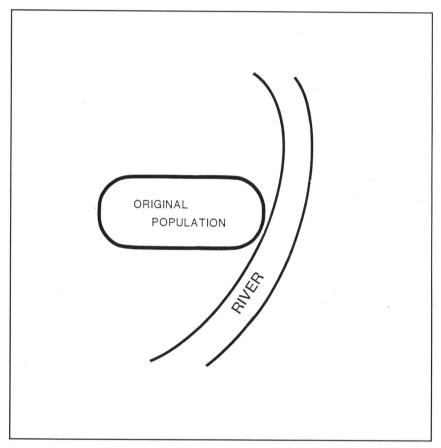

Figure 1. Original population next to river.

(A) *Geographic barriers.* Figure 1 illustrates a situation where a population of organisms of the same species exists alongside a river. Let us suppose that a flood occurred and, when the river receded, it had changed its course somewhat (Figure 2).

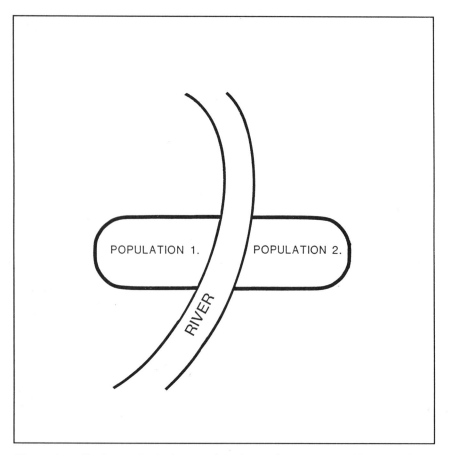

Figure 2. Following a flood, the river has changed its course and has split the original population.

The result of this was that the original population was split into two smaller populations. The individuals in these two populations are still in the same species — they are *potentially* able to interbreed, but they cannot actually interbreed because (we will suppose) they cannot get across the river. The story continues as we now understand that population 1 has mutations, recombinations, and natural selection occurring which are independent of the mutations, recombinations, and natural selection occurring in population 2. In other words, changes are occurring in the individuals in population 1 which are not shared by interbreeding with individuals in population 2 and vice versa. We might envision, for instance, that the environments of the two populations are different because prevailing winds make more rainfall on one side of the river or there are predators on one side but not the other. It is not hard to envision how the two populations might face different environments, and thus different natural selection pressures.

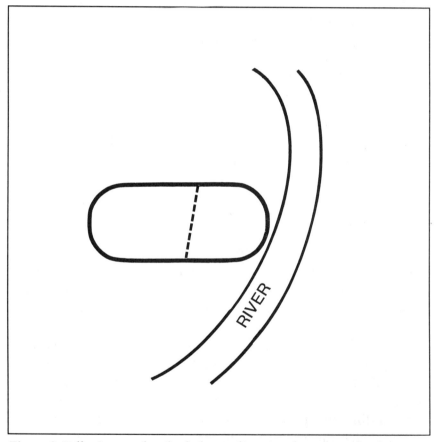

Figure 3. Following another flood, the receding river has returned to its original channel.

Figure 3 illustrates that another flood has occurred and now, when the river receded, it went back to its original channel.

Now the organisms can once again get to one another, but the idea goes, the two groups have now been changing (evolving) independently for so long that when they do get together they cannot interbreed. They have changed from one another enough that the interbreeding process cannot occur. Because they cannot now breed together they are in different species, and speciation has occurred.

An assumption with this technique of reproductive isolation is that a significant amount of time has elapsed during which the original population was split. Nevertheless, the idea is very attractive to many biologists and can include not only flood situations but such events as fires, lava flows, earthquakes, and eruption of hills and mountains as geographic barriers.

(B) *Exaggerated Variability.* This technique of reproductive isolation simply suggests that, since individuals in a species vary from one another and that the variation is continually being added to by mutations and recombinations, it is conceivable that there will come a time when the variation is so great that organisms at the extremes will not be able to reproduce.

Figure 4 illustrates a situation considering the body size of some hypothetical animal. Most of the animals in this species are of an average size, but there are a few extremes of large or small animals. The curve represents the variation of body sizes and the ends (extremes) are continually being pushed to the left and right by mutations and recombinations. The idea is that one can envision a time when the extremely large animals simply cannot mate with the extremely small animals. If and when that occurs, the organisms are reproductively isolated and are in a different species. Notice that no single factor has occurred which causes the organisms to be unable to interbreed; they simply have become so different from one another that something in the reproductive process is insufficient. In this hypothetical example the body size difference makes the organisms simply physically incapable. Exampless might compare

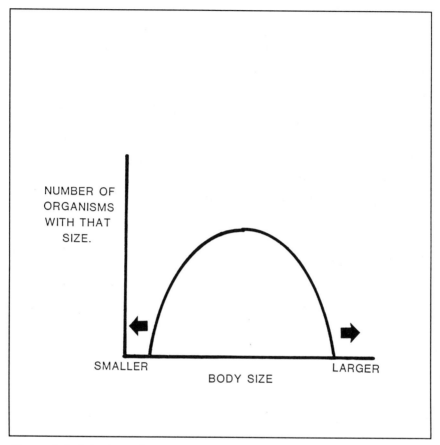

Figure 4. Original population next to river.

bullfrogs to grassfrogs or tigers to housecats. Size is certainly not the only factor of consideration here. Perhaps even more likely would be reproductive timing (pollen from plants must be available at the same time as the eggs) or premating behavior in animals.

Speciation is, thus, thought to occur by reproductive isolation occurring in groups of organisms subjected to mutations, recombinations, and natural selection. Is the idea valid?

It is important here to return to our understanding of science as being able to deal with observable, measurable events. As I indicated before, there are many experiments showing that mutations, recombinations, and natural selection are solid ideas and scientists clearly accept them as fact. Reproductive isolation is somewhat more difficult to illustrate because of the longer time factors involved. But still, I believe, the vast majority of biologists believe that it occurs. There are pieces of evidence that indicate situations where one species is *in the process of splitting* and other situations where a split must have just relatively recently occurred.

For example, in the Grand Canyon the Kaibab squirrel inhabits the north side and the Abert squirrel inhabits the south side. The squirrels are very similar but do have some differences (for instance, in fur color) and apparently are largely restricted from interbreeding because they do not cross the Grand Canyon. Interested biologists believe the squirrels are derived from the same ancestor line, but the biologists do not agree whether the squirrels have reached the level of two full species or whether they should still be considered well-marked variants of a single species; in other words, the reproductive isolation process may not be complete yet.

One other example may be helpful. The hawthorne fly is an insect pest which originally infested only native hawthorne fruits in the northwestern United States. In 1864 cultivated apple trees planted near the native hawthornes were suddenly infested by a sub-group of the hawthorne fly population. Then, in 1960, a sub-group of the apple infesting group shifted to adjacent orchards planted with cherry trees. Because cherries ripen earlier in the year than apples, these two sub-groups of the original hawthorne fly are reproductively isolated. This is because the adult flies of the two groups emerge and breed at different times in the summer.

Despite the apparent triviality of such situations, they are samples of reproductive isolation. It would seem that the evidence for speciation is clear; it can be observed to be occurring, and, thus is a scientifically valid explanation for part of the diversity of life.

Problems arise, however, it seems to me, when we attempt to take the mechanisms of speciation (which are rather clearly correct, I believe) and let them be responsible for all the diversity we see in life. Some would make this argument: If one species can split into two by these mechanisms, why cannot larger groupings of organisms (even phyla and classes) be understood to have evolved in the same way, only using much longer time periods? The only difference between a species splitting in two and a class splitting in two would be a much longer time for mutations, recombinations, natural selection, and reproductive isolation to occur. To a great many biologists the logic of this thought is clear. But just because an idea seems to be logical does not mean that it is necessarily correct.

My own view is that "evolution" has gotten a lot more "press" than it deserves. People tend to get "hobbies" and think the world revolves around some particular idea or activity. It might be baseball, musical performance, capitalism, or even — evolution.

On one hand, there are biologists who make it their personal cause to make all of biology have evolutionary implications. To many scientists evolution theory is a very helpful unifying concept, and it is important that biologists understand and appreciate its implications, but there is a great deal of fundamental biology which is useful and interesting in its own right regardless of its connection to evolution.

On the other hand, there is no reason for anyone to be staggered at the fact that there is clear evidence which could support evolution at one level (speciation), and to extend that to more major groups seems plausible. I said at the beginning that I wanted to help a reader understand why evolution theory is so attractive to so many scientists. Here we are at a summary statement: Many scientists feel that the *observations* which support evolution or change at the *species* level lead to the conclusion that change at *every* level (even the major groups) is due to the same factors. To many, this is a logical extension of the speciation idea. It is important to remember that a scientist is looking for an explanation which best satisfies the available observations..

The next point is particularly important, however. Despite observations supporting *species* changes, in our lifetime spans we do not observe *major groups* changing. To make the extension of speciation to more major groups requires faith.

Faith may be an odd addition to a discussion of evolution, but I am amazed at how reluctant people are to consider it. Whatever one's particular stance on "how life forms got to where they are today," as one goes back in time one moves from certainty (what is clearly observable and measurable) to uncertainty (what is not clearly observable and measurable) at some point. At this point one becomes a person of faith. None of us is completely logical and objective. Each of us has a personal history and our view of events in our lives and what we learn become meaningful in the light of our personal history. This is different from bias or wishful thinking; it is simply recognizing that all of us have limited insight and, to a great extent, are the products of our own personal experiences.

My own faith leads me to be very impressed with the efficiency and balance of life, even of my own body, and to admit that it is unreasonable to suggest that it all came about by random processes. Other aspects of my faith teach me that there are purposes in life and it all comes together for me to indicate that there was, and is, a Creator. I believe, as a scientist, in mechanisms which introduce and evaluate change in life, but I will join Albert Einstein in suggesting that the intricacies of life and nature cause a "... deeply emotional conviction of the presence of a superior reasoning power...."

For the sake of completeness, let me add one more scientific note. I have explained the basics of evolution theory as it is commonly considered, that is, as occurring in a long, smooth, gradual process. In recent years there have been some scientists who have suggested that the process has, indeed, occurred over a long time period, but that the changes have occurred in "bursts" within that time period.

The fossil record shows few transition situations. That is, new species appear in the fossil record rather abruptly and then undergo little observable change for the rest of their existence. This has commonly been explained as simply an indication of the *incompleteness* of the fossil record. Another interpretation of this, however, is that speciation has occurred by "jumps." There are possible observable biologic events which could cause a dramatic change in a species and this, coupled with an environmental crisis of some sort causing strong natural selection, could lead to speciation in a relatively short period of time. This "relatively short period of time," however, would be in the thousands of years, possibly even 100,000 years. But this is still significantly more rapid than speciation has been traditionally thought to occur.

This speciation by "bursts," or "punctuated equilibrium," as it is called, represents a modification of evolutionary theory but does not suggest changes in the mechanisms thought to *cause* speciation. It should also not be taken as evidence that evolutionists "cannot agree among themselves" and, therefore, adds further discredit to evolution. Scientists in any field *expect* to disagree over the interpretation of the available observations.

5

COMPARATIVE ANATOMY AND EMBRYOLOGY AS SOURCES OF EVIDENCE FOR EVOLUTION

CLARK STEVENS

*P*ublication in 1858 of Darwin's book entitled *On the Origin of the Species by Means of Natural Selection* initiated a tremendous surge of interest in and acceptance of the doctrine of evolution. This work also provided great impetus to biological investigation, primarily in search of evidence to support the theory of evolution and to discover lines of evolutionary descent. In spite of the restricted goals of the search, much interesting and important information was uncovered.

Many scientists attribute to Darwin much of the inspiration for most of the major developments in modern biological and medical sciences. Probably more credit is given to him than he actually merits. Comparative anatomy and embryology are two fields of study in biology which were especially amplified under the impetus of the Darwinian movement. It was generally conceded that these two fields were rich in evidence of the highest order supporting the fact of evolution and probably were among the best sources of information for mapping lines of evolutionary descent.

The structure of plants and animals was already being used extensively before Darwin's time as a means for classifying living forms. Most classification groups had already been defined on the basis of similarity in structural characteristics. Little or no evolutionary significance had been associated with this earlier classification because evolution had not yet been popularly accepted. After Darwin's hypothesis, similarity in structure was assumed by many to be the best evidence for common lines of evolutionary descent. On this assumption comparative anatomists began to gather evidence in earnest. Two main lines of attack were employed: the study of homology (likeness) of parts and the search for vestigial (rudimentary) organs in modern organisms.

Homologous organs are those with corresponding parts and similar embryonic origin in the different organisms. Some homologies in current organisms are easy to establish. For example, the wing of a bat, the flipper of a whale, the leg of a dog, and the arm of a human are homologous. Although differing in functions and having different superficial structure, these organs do have the same pattern of bone structure and they share a common pattern of embryologic development. Numerous other homologies have been compiled and have been offered as positive proof of the evolutionary descent of modern organisms from ancestral organisms with similar homologous organs.

Vestigial organs are rudimentary structures without known function. Supposedly they are evolutionary traces of ancestral organs which did have useful functions. Intensive search for vestigial organs has resulted in the compilation of long lists of these structures in various kinds of organisms. Assumption generally has been made that only evolution can provide an explanation for such organs. Hence, discovery of a vestigial organ has been considered as a definite proof of evolution. Vestigial organs reported in man include the following: pineal gland, pituitary gland, thymus gland, thyroid gland, parathyroid glands, tonsils, adenoids, spleen, cecum, appendix, and such embryonic structures as aortic arches, yolk sac, allantois, and "gill slits." Even a superficial examination of this list will reveal that most cannot be recognized any longer as rudimentary because definite functions have been established for them. In fact, some even have vital functions. However, establishing vital function is not essential in order to delete an organ from the list of vestigial organs.

Comparative anatomy no longer occupies an exalted position as "queen of the sciences" for gathering evidence in favor of evolution. The greatest weakness of the evidence from comparative anatomy is the false premise upon which it is based: that is, "similarity in the structure of different organisms can only logically be explained on the basis of common evolutionary origin." This explanation is no more logical than one based on an origin by creation through the purposeful acts of a Divine Creator. Different organisms created with overall structural similarities (such as the mammals) should be expected to share many organs which have corresponding parts and which have undergone similar embryological development (homologous organs).

A second major problem facing the comparative anatomist is to prove that homologous organs are actually ancestral in origin. It cannot be concluded with any certainty that organs are ancestral unless a common ancestor which possesses these organs is discovered. Oftentimes no appropriate fossil can be discovered. The ancestor is only hypothetical. Furthermore, sometimes parallel mutations (chemical changes in genes) and parallel variations occur in two different organisms, which cause homologous organs to develop that did not previously occur in either family line. Hence, it is not easy to determine always whether an organ is "recent or ancestral." In addition, study of specializations in these organs presents evidence which distorts the picture of evolution or perhaps even contradicts major opinions as to its course. Determining relative phylogenetic ages of two kinds of organisms by comparing the degree of specialization in their homologous organs yields various results, depending upon which organs are selected for comparison. The more specialized an organ has become, the more recently it is supposed to have evolved. One organism may have an organ which is considered to be more primitive (less specialized) than a homologous organ in another organism, even though the former organism is believed to be more recently evolved than the latter on the basis of other comparisons. This gets to be quite confusing. Some modern anatomists caution against trying to apply anatomical evidence rigidly because it does become confusing.

The weight of evidence suppporting the fact of evolution derived from the study of vestigial organs also has diminished considerably as the list of real vestigial organs has been progressively reduced. Almost all of those human organs originally identified as vestigial have proved to be functional organs. Furthermore, it is now well known that structures important to embryonic development may persist after birth without apparent function. Other embryonic organs serve their roles and then disappear. Still others serve important roles after birth.[1] Organs with developmental functions should not be classified as true vestigial organs. That all organs originally classified as vestigial may ultimately prove to be functional organs is quite possible. Proving that evolution has occurred by citing the occurrence of vestigial organs is no longer very convincing.

The other important line of biological research for evidence supporting the fact of evolution has been embryological. In 1868, Ernst Haeckel formulated the theory of recapitulation or the biogenetic law. According to this theory, an organism in its individual development (ontogeny) passes through (recapitulates) the sequence of stages in its evolution (phylogeny). Thus, the motto of evolutionists for half a century or longer was, "Ontogeny recapitulates phylogeny." Haeckel was especially fascinated by the similarity of development in the embryos of all vertebrates (animals with backbones). Each fertilized egg was visualized by him to be the stage of a onc-celled animal (protozoan). Each egg typically undergoes multiple divisions which to him was equivalent to a colony of one-celled animals. Rearrangement of these cells then produces a stage which he thought represented the jelly-fish group of animals. Growth in the length of the "jelly-fish stage" results in a "worm-like stage." Subsequent development of the embryo does not produce stages which he could recognize as evolutionary stages. Nevertheless, he was confident that embryological development was tracing the course of the evolution of the species. Although he could not recognize definite ancestral stages in the late development of vertebrate embryos, he was convinced that certain organs or organ systems in the late embryos were representative of ancestral recapitulations. Various structures develop in the human embryo, for example, which resemble to some extent adult structures in certain of the "lower animals," although these structures are not retained in the same form in the human afterbirth. These especially develop in association with the respiratory system, the circulatory system, and the excretory system. These have been classified by Haeckel and his disciples as ancestral structures and they have been accepted by him as strong evidence for the truth of evolution.

As impressive as these alleged examples of recapitulation appear to be, later detailed studies have progressively sapped the theory of its erstwhile viability as a broad generalization of importance in biology. Decades ago most embryological texts devoted considerable space to recapitulation, usually an entire chapter. Modern texts hardly mention the theory. Some make no mention at all. Furthermore, ontogeny and phylogeny are words that do not even appear in the index of many texts. Although sometimes embryologic descriptions are still based on the premise of recapitulation, little emphasis is given to that aspect. Even by 1931, recapitulation was already recognized by embryologists as only partial truth.[2] But it had fallen from the exalted position of "a general law of nature" to a lowly "possible trend." Other embryologists have still espoused the theory, but they have cautioned against using it too rigidly in the study of evolution because of its distortion of the picture of ancestral history.[3] This distortion supposedly was imposed by the brevity of the developmental period. This brevity had made necessary the shortening of stages, the omission of some stages, the rearrangement of other stages, and the alteration of the relative lengths of most stages. The possibility of interpolation of new stages at any point in the developmental sequence had proved to be even more confusing. By 1967, Charles K. Weichert [4] asserted in his popular textbook of comparative anatomy that all biologists know now that recapitulation does not actually occur, even though similarity in the development of vertebrate animals does exist. Arthur S. Hopper and Nathan H. Hart [5] have concurred in Weichert's assertion and have affirmed further that the human embryo is always clearly human. They clearly state that it is never the counterpart of a "fish stage" or of the stage of any other animal.

What has befallen this once mighty "general law of nature" (law of biogenesis)? The primary weakness of its "evidence" lies in the false premise that similarity of development can be explained logically only by evolutionary relationship. Actually the same similarity in development would be expected in relationship by creation. Two different kinds of organisms created with similar adult structures (such as the mammals) would be expected to have similar developmental patterns.

Another weakness of recepitulation is the distorted picture of evolutionary history that it presents. If the proposed evolutionary stages can be abbreviated, omitted, or sequentially rearranged in embryological development, then little weight can be given to the picture presented. Furthermore, its evidence is worthless if new stages can be interpolated at any point in the sequence of developmental stages.

Recapitulations which involve only certain organs or organ systems, rather than entire stages, also pose a problem to the evolutionist. These recapitulations have lost much of their former impact as evidence for the fact of evolution because of the discovery that most (and probably all) play vital roles in embryological development. They cannot be treated as mere recapitulations of ancestral organs because their presence in the developing embryo is essential for normal development. It has been previously noted that embryological structures with vital roles in development undergo various fates after their roles are completed. Some disappear altogether. Others persist in rudimentary form without further known function. Still others persist after birth but assume different functions. One must not conclude, however, that any of these organs are just useless recapitulations of evolutionary history.

At one time recapitulation of ancestral stages in individual development was cited with great confidence as evidence for an evolutionary origin for modern organisms. Citing recapitulation today as evidence for the fact of evolution is not very impressive. The validity of this once broad generalization has been greatly undermined. Considering its broad application in times past to the animal kingdom, it now seems strikingly odd that little indication of it has been reported in the plant kingdom. As major sources of evidence which support the fact of evolution, embryology and comparative anatomy have both been "weighed in the balances and found wanting."

By way of summary, the evidence presented from both fields has been based on the premise that similarities in different kinds of organisms (either in structure or in development) can be logically explained only by the evolutionary relationship of the organisms. Hence, the evidence presented has been chiefly descriptions of similarities. Great significance has been attached in time past to homologous organs shared by many different kinds of organisms. Homologous organs are those with corresponding parts and similar embryological development. Similar homologous organs which might be discovered in fossil forms supposedly would seal the evolutionary relationship. Much effort in comparative anatomy has also been expended in identifying vestigial organs, which are defined as traces of ancestral organs retained without function in modern organisms. Supposedly the homologous ancestral organs had definite functions.

In embryology, most of the evidence to support the fact of evolution has been concerned with Haeckel's theory of recapitulation (the law of biogenesis) which states that the individual in its development passes through the various stages of evolutionary development. For many years strong beliefs existed and high hopes were felt that the evolutionary history of each kind of modern organism would ultimately be revealed in its embryological development.

In years gone by, the findings in comparative anatomy and embryology have caused great waves of excitement in those who espouse the cause of evolution. The evidence inferred has been proclaimed loudly and with flourish. However, in current times, such findings hardly cause a ripple of excitement and the evidence inferred is usually proclaimed rather cautiously. What has caused the loss in significance of the evidence from these two fields? The principal factors are the following:

1. The assumption that evolutionary relationship is the only logical explanation for the similarities in organisms is false. Relationship by creation is just as logical.

2. Homologous structures do not necessarily imply relationship in the family lines of organisms.

3. Repeated failures in the search among fossils for the ancestors hypothesized for modern organisms has been a great hindrance in establishing evolutionary relations.

4. The long lists of "vestigial organs" compiled in the past have been reduced to almost none as definite functions have been progressively found for most of the organs.

5. The vital evidence provided by embryology has been devitalized by the belated recognition that recapitulation of evolutionary stages during embryological development does not actually occur.

Anatomical and embryological evidence that modern life forms have evolved from a common ancestor is weak, confusing, and in some instances even conflicting. Faith in creation by a living God should not be weakened to any extent when such evidence is considered carefully.

N O T E S

1. A.S.Hopper and N.H.Hart, *Foundations of Animal Development,* Oxford University Press, 1980, p. 5.

2. A.Richards, *Outline of Comparative Embryology,* John Wiley and Sons, New York: 1931, p.290.

3. B.M.Patten, *Embryology of the Pig,* The Blakiston Company, Philadelphia 1948, p. 174.

4. C.K.Weichert, *Elements of Chordate Anatomy,* 3rd Ed., New York: McGraw Hill, 1967, p.5.

5. Hopper and Hart, op. cit., pp. 4,5.

6

FROM THE DUST OF THE EARTH...

PERRY C. REEVES

*B*y his very nature man is very curious. Observations, such as the appearance of an abundance of croaking frogs in muddy creek beds after rains, caused our ancestors to ponder the source of life and eventually led them to propose the theory of spontaneous generation. This theory, which suggested that some species of animals arose spontaneously from mud, grain, or decaying matter, counted Aristotle as one of its major supporters. Scientific giants of the past such as William Harvey and Sir Isaac Newton were also believers in this theory. In the early 1600's, the noted Belgian physician, van Helmont wrote: "If a dirty undergarment is squeezed into the mouth of a vessel containing wheat, within a few days, 21 is a critical period, the ferment drained from the garment and transformed by the smell of the grain encrusts the wheat itself with its own skin and turns it into mice."

The first to test this belief by careful experimentation was the Italian physician Francesco Redi. In 1668, he established that maggots in decaying meat had arisen from microscopically small fly eggs rather than from the meat itself. Despite this demonstration, the belief in the possibility of spontaneous generation of microorganisms remained very much alive. Two centuries later in 1862, Louis Pasteur finally destroyed this theory when he demonstrated that microorganisms were transported by air and were not spontaneously generated in sterile media. His "germ theory" suggested that "life begets life."

Within the last few years, a modern version of spontaneous generation has arisen. This new theory suggests that the elements present at the beginning of the universe have been transformed in an orderly sequence from atoms to small molecules, to larger molecules, to cells, and finally to life as we know it. This chapter is devoted to a brief review of this new hypothesis which has been termed "chemical evolution."

> Then God said, "Let us make man in our image, in our likeness, and let them rule over the fish of the sea and the birds of the air, over the livestock, over all the earth, and over all the creatures that move along the ground." — *GENESIS 1:26....*
>
> Then "the Lord God formed the man from the dust of the ground and breathed into his nostrils the breath of life, and the man became a living being." — *GENESIS 2:7....*

What amazing chemistry is described in these two verses of scripture! As Adam stood in the garden on his first day of life, he was surely not a mere clay mannequin but was a living being composed of a vast array of complex chemical molecules — just like you and I. Today we know that living things are composed of proteins, carbohydrates, lipids, nucleic acids, as well as inorganic materials and water. However, a relatively small number of chemical components are needed to transmit all of the genetic information that accounts for the rich variety of life that exists of the earth today. The nucleic acids (DNA and RNA) carry a genetic code that completely describes each one of us; yet, these complex molecules are constructed from only eight building blocks. These materials are five organic bases (adenine, thymine, guanine, cytosine, uracil), two simple sugars (ribose, deoxyribose), and a phosphate group. The genetic information is "translated" and "transcribed" to produce proteins. Proteins have a myriad of functions. As enzymes and hormones, they catalyze and regulate the reactions that occur in the body; as muscles and tendons they enable the body to move; as skin and hair they give it a covering; as hemoglobin they transfer all-important oxygen to each cell; as antibodies they provide it with a defense mechanism against disease; and in combination with other substances in bone they provide it with structural support. Despite this diversity of function, these proteins are constructed from only 20 simple units called amino acids. Therefore, a total of only 28 building blocks is needed to construct the two most important types of molecules associated with all living creatures — from the largest mammal to the smallest microbe. This alphabet of life has only two more "letters" than the English alphabet, and the "words" that can be written using it are truly marvelous.

Did the Great Creator instantly transform the "dust of the earth" into these essential chemical molecules of life, or did they simply arise through natural physical processes over eons of time? Many scientists favor this last view of the origin of life, and since 1950 much research has focused on the laboratory production of these molecules under "early earth" conditions.

In 1952, Stanley Miller, a first year graduate student at the University of Chicago, performed what has become a classical experiment in the field of chemical evolution. Electric discharges were passed through a mixture of methane, ammonia, hydrogen, and water vapor for a period of one week. These materials had been chosen because the Russian scientist Alexander Oparin had proposed in 1924 that they were the components of the early earth atmosphere. Miller found that the reaction had produced many organic molecules — among which were four or five of the common amino acids found in living systems. He postulated that this experiment simulated the conditions under which "chemical evolution" had begun.

By the 1970's, the scientific community had changed its theories about the composition of the early earth's atmosphere because of data collected by NASA's probes to other planets. However, scientists using different energy sources such as ultraviolet light, heat, and electron beams along with different combinations of gases also produced mixtures of organic compounds, including some of the common amino acids.

In 1970, Dr.Cyril Ponnamperuma reported the first evidence for extraterrestrial amino acid production when he described the results of chemical analysis of a type of 2,000 meteorites in museum collections around the world and of these approximately 4% are carbonaceous chondrites. These meteorites contain small amounts (less than 6% by weight) of organic compounds. His analysis revealed the presence of a large number of amino acids and furthermore demonstrated that they were not the result of contamination from living materials on the earth. Similar results were found when other carbonaceous chondrites were analyzed. This led some scientists to propose that meteorites contributed a substantial portion of the amino acids available for the emergence of life on earth.

Living systems link amino acids into long chains to form proteins; therefore, several groups began to search for a pre-biotic route to proteins. In 1958, Dr. Sidney Fox found that intermediate-sized "proteinoids" were obtained in dry-phase heating experiments or by heating concentrated solutions of amino acids. Other researchers repeated the experiments with the amino acids absorbed on clay surfaces with similar results. These conditions were chosen to simulate the evaporation of ponds to dryness or near dryness as the theoretical primordial ocean receded. The "proteinoids" exhibited a few properties of cells and were hailed as examples of "protocells."

The story as told so far seems to indicate that this process is all very reasonable and possible; however, there are difficulties that haven't been addressed. In detailed studies of the Murchison meteorite and Miller's electric discharge experiments, at least 30 different amino acids have been identified, but the vast majority of living organisms utilize no more than 22 amino acids. If life evolved in this manner why aren't some of these other amino acids found in living systems, since they were obviously available for incorporation into the "protocells"?

A second problem involves the unique three-dimensional structure of amino acids. The common amino acids (with the exception of glycine) can orient their atoms in two arrangements differing only in that one arrangement is the mirror-image of the other. A simple example of this phenomenon is the relationship between your two hands. Your left hand and right hand are identical in the manner in which the parts are connected, but your left hand is the mirror-image of the right hand! No matter how hard you try you cannot superimpose one of your hands upon upon the other.

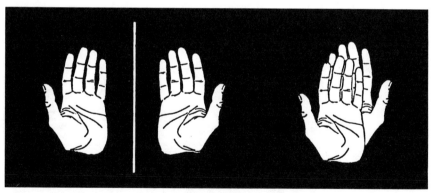

The left hand is a mirror-image of the right hand. The left and right hands are not superimposable.

Another way to think of this is to compare yourself with the image in your own mirror. You are identical in all ways except that when you have a freckle on your left cheek the image in the mirror has a freckle on the right cheek! Does this sound strange? Check it out for yourself. This property of molecules is called "optical activity" and these molecules are said to be "chiral." Why is this important? Chiral molecules react differently in biological systems. For example, does it matter which one of a pair of gloves you try to put on your left hand? Have you ever tried to put a right-hand glove on your left hand? It doesn't work very well. The same thing is true in biological systems. If your try to incorporate a "right-handed" amino acid into a protein system, it doesn't work; however, a "left-handed" amino acid is readily accepted. With minor exceptions all of the living systems utilize "left-handed" amino acids exclusively. That must indicate that all of the amino acids produced in the "early earth" simulations are of this "left-handed" type! However, the experimental facts fail to bear this out. All of the amino acids produced in the laboratory or found in meteorites are equal mixtures of the "left-" and "right-handed" forms.

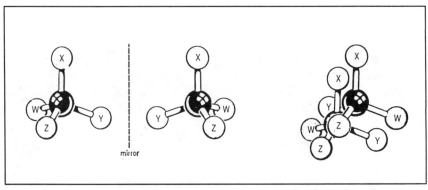

Ball and stick models showing non-superimposable molecules such as the amino acids.

Researchers have suggested that polarized light or chiral radiation produced by radioactive decay might have selectively destroyed the "right-handed" forms or that the earth's rotation in a magnetic field influenced molecular reactivity. The conclusion of several participants at a chemical evolution symposium in 1983 was that they still didn't understand how chirality evolved. In fact some of them suggested that the whole matter be dropped because it was an experimentally unsolvable problem. Could it be that these phenomena didn't happen simply by chance?

A third problem concerns the complex nature of proteins. It is estimated that the human body contains over 100,000 different protein molecules ranging in size from small ones containing only a few amino acid units to very large ones containing more than a thousand units. A typical protein contains anywhere from 100 to 300 amino acid units. If one were to think of a protein as a word and the amino acid units as letters in that word, the question arises, "Does it matter what letters are used and in what order they come?" The answer is obvious to anyone who is learning to spell, but it is also important in protein structure as well.

The following examples illustrate the importance of sequence and composition in some proteins found in the human body. Oxytocin and vasopressin are two simple proteins produced by the pituitary gland. If one replaces only two of the nine amino acid units in oxytocin with other amino acid, vasopressin results. This minor change in composition results in markedly different physiological effects in the body. Oxytocin causes contraction of smooth muscles and thus aids in childbirth. On the other hand, vasopressin causes a rise in blood pressure and regulates excretion of water by the kidneys. The importance of correct composition and order of the amino acid units is shown even more dramatically in the case of hemoglobin. This protein contains four separate chains and each chain contains more than 100 amino acid units. The substitution of one incorrect amino acid in only two of the four chains drastically alters the functioning of the molecule, and results in a sometimes-fatal condition known as "sickle-cell anemia." Many other examples could be given but these should suffice to demonstrate that the composition of proteins is very critical. When one examines the vast number of possible structures that could result from a simple random combination of amino acid units in an evaporating primordial pond, it is mind-boggling to believe that life could have originated in this way. It is more plausible that a Great Builder with a master plan would be required for such a task.

In living systems, the production of protein is governed by RNA and DNA, which are commonly called the nucleic acids. Since the nucleic acids are so closely connected with proteins, researchers are faced with the "which came first — the chicken or the egg?" question. Most of them now believe that the nucleic acids were formed first. The nucleic acids are very large molecules which transmit the genetic code. Nucleotides are the fundamental sub-units of nucleic acids in the same manner that amino acids are the sub-units of proteins. Nucleotides are made up of sugars (ribose in RNA, deoxyribose in DNA), organic bases (pyrimidines, purines), and inorganic phosphate groups.

Research groups have been somewhat successful in producing the sugars and bases in the laboratory. They use as starting materials the well-known substances formaldehyde and hydrogen cyanide. The question is — "Could these materials have been present on an 'early earth?'" Astronomers have now detected these and many more molecules in interstellar space, in comets, and on the surfaces of other bodies in our solar system. Other possible sources from reactions on earth itself have been simulated in the laboratory.

In the 1960's workers at the Salk Institute demonstrated that one could produce amino acids, purines, and pyrimidines by reactions of concentrated hydrogen cyanide (HCN) solutions at low temperatures (-5 degrees Fahrenheit). However, it is not at all apparent how these concentrated solutions could have accumulated on an early earth. Attempts to concentrate dilute solutions by evaporation of the water results in the loss of HCN instead. Therefore scenarios involving evaporation of the primordial seas are not plausible. Instead the Salk workers proposed a scenario involving the freezing of primitive seas during harsh winters to provide the concentrations and temperatures needed.

The required sugars can be formed by reactions of formaldehyde in the presence of metal ions normally found in clays and seawater. However, there are several problems with this model. In addition to ribose and deoxyribose, a complex mixture of other sugars is also formed. In fact, the desired sugars are only a very minor portion of the total reaction product. Moreover, the desired sugars are prone to destruction under the conditions of the experiment. Nevertheless, this is the current model that is most favored.

Once one has assembled the smallest building blocks, the question arises — "How are they combined into the nucleotides and then into the nucleic acids?" Once again the evaporating sea is the preferred model. The heating of dry mixtures of purines, sugar, and inorganic phosphates in the presence of magnesium or calcium ions leads to the formation of nucleotides. These nucleotides then link up to form short chains which could be viewed as very elementary forms of the nucleic acids. However, an important difficulty with this experiment is that the pyrimidine bases will not undergo this reaction, yet they constitute approximately half of the organic bases found in nucleic acids. One area of current interest involves finding ways to accomplish the same chemical reactions in water, thereby simulating conditions in an ancient sea.

Could random combination of the nucleotides into nucleic acids have produced the variety of life we see today? I believe not! The genetic code is based upon the correct sequence of these individual units. A sequence of 3 nucleotide units is required to specify one amino acid in the protein. Therefore a simple protein such as insulin (involved in metabolism of carbohydrates) would require that at least 153 nucleotide units be arranged in the correct order. If this order was not present, a different substance would be produced. It is extremely difficult for me to believe (and also mathematically improbable) that this could have happened by a simple trial and error chance process.

While the scientists studying chemical evolution have had some success in the laboratory, they are faced with a great number of unsolved questions. First, where did the chemical elements and substances which they use to begin their process originate? They cannot begin with nothing, but we believe that God spoke the universe into existence out of nothing! Secondly, if the evolution of life is simply the result of the workings of the natural and physical laws of the universe, there should be life in other parts of the universe. Some scientists have estimated that there are millions of other bodies within the universe that have conditions suitable for the evolution of life. Yet despite years of intense "listening to the skies" for radio signals from outer space and searching for life on other planets in our solar system, no evidence for life has been found except on planet Earth. Should simple or complex life forms someday be found elsewhere in the universe, it would still not prove that life originally appeared as the result of only blind chance!

Is God's way, man's way? What if man someday produces a complete cell in the laboratory? Does that destroy faith in God's creative acts? It certainly should not. The following quotation from Dr. Rod O'Connor in his textbook, *Fundamentals of Chemistry*, summarizes the beliefs of many of us who are both scientists and Christians:

> As research in the field of molecular biology progresses, the temptation for scientists to be overly impressed by their own knowledge is almost overwhelming. It has become possible within the last 25 years to produce common organic molecules by electric discharge (simulating lightning) through gas mixtures like those believed to constitute the atmosphere of the primitive earth. Mixtures of amino acids heated on powdered rock and quenched by cooling rains (simulated) have formed polypeptides whose macrostructures are similar to those of

many proteins. Synthetic nucleic acids have demonstrated the self-replicating properties of their natural relatives. Do these and other similar developments prove the theories of the accidental origin of life? One might believe so from many current texts and classes.

However, it is important to realize the limitations of scientific investigation. By its nature, science requires observation and investigation. It is possible to determine one or more routes by which an event may now occur. It is not possible to determine through science the unique way in which an event took place at a time before observations were made. No reputable scientist would dream of picking up a strange sample of alanine and, from his knowledge of synthetic chemistry, stating as fact exactly how that particular sample was made. The same scientist might find it difficult to resist the impulse to state rather dogmatically the route by which complex life forms evolved on the primitive earth.

There is no reason for scientists to discard a belief in God. Indeed, there are many who feel the need for a faith that suggests human life is more than a series of chemical changes and that it need not end when some of these reactions cease. The belief in the existence of a soul, a way in which a life ought to be lived, and a life beyond this transient one cannot be subjected to scientific tests. At worst, such a belief is a harmless fantasy. If true, and many of us are convinced that it is, it is far more important than anything science, technology, or this world has to offer.

NOTES

I. Asminov, "Asminov's Guide to Science," New York: Basic Books, Inc., 1972, pp.624-638.

S.J.Baum, "Introduction to Organic and Biological Chemistry," 2nd Ed., New York: Macmillan, 1978, pp.330-431. (Has general information on proteins, enzymes and nucleic acids).

H.G.Coffin, "Creation, The Evidence From Science.," (This panphlet may be obtained from Life Origins Foundation, Box 277, Anacortes, Washington, 98221).

J.P.Ferris, "The Chemistry of Life's Origin," in *Chemical and Engineering News*, August 27, 1984, pp. 22-35.

K.McDonald, "Growing Body of Evidence Indicates Life Began in a Chemical Process Common in the Universe," in *Chronicle of Higher Education*, October 8, 1986, pp. 6-9.

S.L.Miller, "A Production of Amino Acids under Possible Primitive Earth Conditions," *Science*, Vol. 117, 1953, pp. 528-529. (The original Experiment in "Chemical Evolution").

C. Ponnamperuma, "Cosmochemistry and the Origin of Life," pp. 137-164, in the Proceedings of the Robert A. Welch Foundation Conferences on Chemical Research, XXI, "Cosmochemistry," which was held in Houston, Texas, November 7-9, 1977. Reprints may be requested from The Robert A. Welch Foundation, 4605 Post Oak Place, Suite 200, Houston Texas, 77027.

7

SCIENTIFIC DATING TECHNIQUES AND THE AGE OF THE UNIVERSE

MICHAEL E. SADLER

*I*n this article I shall present some of the physical evidence that indicates that our universe, galaxy, and solar system have great age. Physical determinations that have been made for these ages are 10 to 20 billion years for the universe, 10 to 15 billion years for our galaxy, and about 5 billion years for our solar system. Even 1 billion years is a tremendous length of time compared to anything to which we can relate in human terms, such as our own lifetime or all of recorded history. However, there are "clocks" which have been ticking for eons that allow scientists to make such determinations with a minimum number of assumptions. More importantly, different techniques give similar results, an essential ingredient to any theory that is to survive the scrutiny of independently thinking scientists.

RADIOACTIVE DATING

A. *Carbon Dating.* The example of radioactive dating that most of us have read about, the decay of the 14C (carbon-14) nucleus, cannot be used to determine ages of more than a few thousand years because of its relatively short half-life of 5700 years. Nevertheless, a review of the processes involved may assist in the understanding of how similar techniques are used with other nuclei which are much longer lived.

Isotopes are nuclei which have the same electronic charge but different masses. Three isotopes of carbon are found in nature: ^{12}C (98.892% of all carbon), ^{13}C (1.108%), and ^{14}C (much less than 0.001%). A neutral carbon atom has six electrons orbiting a nucleus which contains six protons and either six, seven or eight neutrons (the isotopes ^{12}C, ^{13}C or ^{14}C, respectively). The superscript preceding the symbol is the mass number and is equal to the sum of protons and neutrons in the nucleus. Both ^{12}C and ^{13}C are stable isotopes, meaning that they do not decay. Because it is unstable, trace amounts of ^{14}C exist in nature only because it is produced continually by nuclear reactions of cosmic rays in the atmosphere. The 14C isotope decays to ^{14}N (nitrogen-^{14}) by emitting an electron and a neutrino, a process called beta emission. The rate for this process, as for all radioactive decays, follows an exponential pattern. This means that a sample of ^{14}C will decay to 1/2 of its original amount in 5700 years. In another 5700 years another 1/2 will decay, leaving 1/4 of the original sample. After another half-life has elapsed (that is, after a total of 17,100 years) we would be left with 1/8 of the original sample, and so on. Since carbon is a constituent of all organic matter, the measured decay of ^{14}C can be used to determine approximately how long ago an organism lived. There is no chemical distinction between the different isotopes of carbon. ^{14}C forms the carbon dioxide ($CO2$) molecule and other organic molecules in the same way as ^{12}C. All organisms living today have the same fraction of ^{14}C (approximately one part in a billion) as is present in nature. When an organism dies, it ceases to ingest carbon so that the fraction of ^{14}C starts to decrease. The dating procedure consists of determining the total carbon content using chemical techniques and then measuring the amount of ^{14}C by detecting the beta radiation. The ratio of ^{14}C to total carbon would be about one part in a billion for contemporary organic material.

If the ratio were found to be one half that in a given sample, the age of the sample would be assumed to be approximately 5700 years.

B. *Dating Using the Heavy Elements.* A method of dating similar in technique to carbon dating is to determine the abundances of heavy elements which decay to lead. Examples are 232Th (Thorium 232, which has a half-life of 14 billion years) and 238U (Uranium-238, with a half-life of 4.5 billion years). Because of their extraordinarily long half-lives these elements still occur in nature. Elements in this mass region trickle down to stable lead isotopes by a chain of decays involving both alpha and beta emission. Reasonable assumptions about the primordial abundances of such elements can be inferred from nuclear properties, such as how tightly the constituent neutrons and protons are bound in the nucleus. The process of determining an age is somewhat more complicated than in carbon dating because of these asssumptions and because of the several steps in the decay chain. However, there are several decay chains which can be studied, providing cross checks on the assumptions. The age of these isotopes has been deduced to be approximately 10 billion years using this technique. This age is the commonly accepted value for all of the chemical elements.

HUBBLE'S LAW AND THE BIG BANG

Other compelling evidence that the universe is very old comes from astronomy. We know that the universe is expanding from measurements of the red shift of the electromagnetic radiation from galaxies. The red shift is so named because red is at the long wavelength end of the visible spectrum and the observed radiation from a receding galaxy is shifted to longer wavelength due to the Doppler effect. The phenomenon can be likened to sound waves being produced by a moving source. An observer can discern when a train whistle has passed him because of this effect. As a train approaches the observed wavelength is shorter (higher frequency) and after the train passes the wavelength is longer (lower frequency). The higher the velocity the larger the shift. Radiation from distant objects called quasars is shifted so much that it is deduced that they are receding from us at a speed approaching that of light.

In addition to being able to measure the speed at which a star or galaxy is receding, astronomers have developed techniques to measure how far certain stars are from us. Distance to the nearby stars can be measured by their parallax, that is, their apparent shifts in position in the night sky as the earth revolves around the sun. The principle is very simple and can be understood by considering two lamps, one which is ten feet away and another which is one mile away. If the observer moves laterally by a few feet, he would have to turn his head appreciably in order to continue looking directly at the closer lamp, but would not have to adjust as much to continue looking at the distant lamp. In the same manner, distant stars appear to be fixed and nearby stars appear to move as the earth revolves around the sun.

Distances that are too great to be measured accurately by the parallax method can be determined indirectly for some pulsating stars which are called Cepheids. These stars have the property that their radiated energy varies in a rhythmic fashion, and the frequency of the variation is correlated with their intrinsic brightness, or absolute magnitude. Stars of the same absolute magnitude would have different apparent magnitudes, depending on how far away the star is from us. The distance of a Cepheid star can then be determined by comparing its apparent magnitude with the absolute magnitude determined from the calibration of brightness as a function of frequency. Distances of far-away galaxies are much more difficult to determine, but can be estimated from their apparent brightness and assuming that they are similar to nearby galaxies.

The interesting result, called Hubble's Law, is that the distances of stars and galaxies correlate with the velocity at which they are receding from us. This correlation is linear, meaning that a galaxy that is twice as far away as another has a velocity that is also larger by a factor of two. The conclusion of all these observations is that all matter in the universe had a common origin, both in space and time. This phenomenon is commonly called the big bang. Assuming that the velocity has always been constant, the age of the universe can be determined from the ratio of the distance to the velocity of the receding stars and galaxies, just as one would calculate how long a trip would take if he knew the distance to be travelled and the average speed at which he planned to drive. The age of the universe is determined to be 10 to 20 billion years by using this technique.

CONCLUSION

Using the techniques described above, experimental evidence indicates that we live in a universe that was created over 10 billion years ago, after which the heavier elements were formed. The age of our solar system is about 4-5 billion years. The uncertainties associated with these ages are sometimes as large as a factor of two, but that still points to ages over a billion years. These conclusions are reached by the same type of scientific investigation that explains how we can get light from flipping a switch or how energy is released in nuclear reactions. The attitude is not supported that such conclusions are only made by misguided scientists who have some satanic vendetta against a deity. Scientists are not all atheists. Indeed, most of the scientists with whom I personally associate believe in God and a Creator.

One of the most overlooked aspects of the big bang theory is that it points to a creation. No known physical process can explain how the enormous amounts of matter and energy necessary for a big bang came into being. This conclusion is further substantiated by the existence of the heavy radioactive elements described above. If the universe had always existed these isotopes would have all decayed. Other evidence for a creation, and hence a Creator, comes from the second law of thermodynamics, which states that energy becomes more disordered as time progresses. If the universe had always existed there would not be any ordered energy left to sustain life.

The major disagreement between scientists and "creationists" (an unfortunate delineation since most scientists accept a creation of some form) is the time element. A valid question then is "what is time?" If God created space and time, along with matter and energy, then how successful can man be in explaining God's creation in terms of time? Time is not an absolute, contrary to our everyday experiences. An example of the non-absoluteness of time is the decay of unstable particles which are moving at velocities which approach the speed of light. Such particles experience longer lifetimes (decay at a slower rate) than particles which are at rest. This phenomenon is predicted by Einstein's theory of relativity and has been confirmed by laboratory measurements. The concept of an eternal God must be of a God who does not exist in time, but has dominion over it. Everything that exists in time becomes more disordered ("runs down") as time passes.

A common explanation of the time discrepancy, if one exists, is that the universe was created with the appearance of age, just as Adam and Eve were created as adults instead of infants. Adherents of a recent creation (i.e, a creation which took place only a few thousand years ago), claim that God would have created trees that already had rings, nuclei which had the appearance of decaying from unstable parent nuclei, and galaxies which obey Hubble's law. This postulate is impossible to refute but it is also impossible to prove. Many believing scientists with whom I interact have difficulty accepting this possibility. An example of a question which comes to mind is "Why would God go to so much trouble to put thousands of yearly ice layers on the polar ice caps?" If the universe were created only a few thousand years ago then light which we now observe from distant galaxies was created in flight and did not originate from the galaxies at all. These galaxies are millions of light years away, where one light year is the distance that light travels in one year. Some participants in the controversy contend that a recent creation would make God deceptive. Adherents to the other point of view answer by stating the completeness by which God created the universe, complete with age, demonstrates his perfectness and supremacy.

A final plea which I would like to make is for acceptance. The Bible does not say how old the earth is, much less the solar system or the universe. To judge as heretics all those who believe that the present universe has evolved from a big bang is unfair and creates controversy over something that is certainly not a central part of Christianity. There is room in the Lord's church for fellowship of people who do not believe exactly alike, as long as we follow the teachings of Christ.

SCIENCE TEACHING AND BIBLE TEACHING

JOE T. ATOR

HE CHALLENGE TO CHRISTIAN TEACHERS OF SCIENCE
Whatever subject a Christian teaches, he should do it in a manner consistent with his religious beliefs whether he is teaching Christians or non-Christians. This presents an interesting challenge in today's enlightened world because of the inevitable clashes between a Christian's understanding of the origin of the universe and the totally mechanistic view of origins held by many modern scientists. Dramatic new discoveries are being announced in areas ranging from the subatomic realm to the realm of the galaxies. A Christian who is also a scientist may view these with reverence because thay deepen his appreciation of the Creator's beneficence and power. But to the scientist who is an agnostic or atheist, they are automatically interpreted in a manner that fits his perception of a mechanical (mindless) universe, where all that is contained in it is a result of the inherent forces of "nature."

A Christian teacher of science is aware of his need to uphold the parallelism between religious truth and scientifically discovered truth. In particular, if his students are Christians, he must prepare them to confront tests of their faith when they enter the professional world. Their faith will likely be challenged in any profession they enter; however, those who plan to enter a scientific profession need to be especially prepared for tests of their belief in the Bible.

A RELATED CONCERN OF BIBLE TEACHERS

There is also a challenge to Bible teachers to properly handle passages dealing with the creation of the universe and all forms of life. It therefore seems appropriate to comment on that topic in connection with the science teaching challenge. A Bible teacher often finds it necessary to teach profound and mind-stretching truths from God's word which appear to be directly in conflict with discoveries or accepted theories being taught in a science course or announced in the news media. Bible class teachers strive to instill faith in the all-powerful, just, and loving God who brought the world, plants, animals and mankind into existence a long time ago. However, if they are familiar with current scientific thought they realize that if their class members should take natural science courses using typical current textbooks, they are likely to experience conflicts if they are encouraged in the Bible class to accept without question unnecessarily restrictive ideas about how and when God shaped our natural world.

What are "unnecessarily restrictive" ideas? In this context, they are those which are not explicitly stated in the Bible, but can be taught by adding words which impose on a Bible passage a restricted meaning in conformance with a preconceived notion. Conflicts may arise between a student's impression about the meaning of a Bible statement and what he is taught in a science course. Of course, valid conflicts may arise when a science book presents as a fact a theory which contradicts clear Bible truth. Conversely, there can be cases where the student's impressions about a Bible statement are confined to one particular meaning not necessarily intended or required by the scripture, and the disturbing effect of an apparently conflicting scientific finding is really unnecessary.

Such is the case with the meaning of the word "day" in scripture where it is used in reference to God's activities in creating the universe. Many analogous examples could be cited in the Bible where words and phrases like "forever," "all the world," "perfect," "every creature," "entire," etc., are used, and commonly accepted exegesis shows that some construed meanings of those words in their context, although not detrimental to the spiritual understanding of the passage, would be inconsistent with truth revealed in other passages or with known facts of history and geography made available to us through God's providence. Usually, as in understanding the meaning of the word "day" in reference to the creation episodes, a reader's initial impression of a word in its contextual sense has no bearing on the intended spiritual message, on the reader's respect for God's word or, indeed, on the validity of New Testament Christianity. We need to be consistent and objective in our application of exegetical principles.

Faith becomes very vulnerable when a greatly detailed, preconceived notion is adopted about what God meant for readers to understand about a given Biblical passage when the scripture does not explicitly include that detailed information. When that is done the reader runs the risk of confronting natural physical evidence in God's universe that is in striking contrast to the preconceived notion. Some try to cope with this dilemma by yielding to the "ostrich effect" . . . they put their head in the sand and pretend the conflict doesn't really exist, or it will go away if they are not directly exposed to it.

In order for man to exercise the dominion over the Earth assigned to him by God he must participate in probing the mysteries and secrets of the universe. Science is a legitimate human enterprise, and Bible teachers should not denigrate it. Virgil Trout states the case well:

> The Christian's attitude towards science must not be either antagonistic or detached. He must interpret science as a discipline of responsibility and privilege of being a good steward of God's creation. He must not view science as a source of evil or as an anti-godly influence.[1]

A Christian who studies science should not fear exposure to ideas that appear to conflict with his understanding of scriptural teaching. When he studies the Bible, he can believe he is studying God's truth, and when he studies or conducts research in a scientific field, he can rest assured that any truth he discovers about natural laws of our universe is something God has allowed him to discover — it is God-provided information for which he should be grateful. Examples of information God has made available for mankind to perceive are radioactive decay rates, depth of the Grand Canyon, distance to the moon, structure of the DNA molecule, the law of gravitation, and the laws of genetics.

If one finds that information gained from a scientific investigation appears to be in conflict with concepts about the world and the universe gained from studying the Bible, he should use the mind God gave him to search out the reason why there is an apparent conflict, to formulate a Christian response to the dilemma, and to decide how to articulate it to others. A Christian student should learn how to face up to such conflicts, with God's help. King Solomon prayed that God would give him "an understanding mind" that he might be able to discern between good and evil (I Kings 3:9), and the inspired writer of the book of Hebrews wrote "solid food is for the mature, for those who have their faculties trained by practice to distinguish good from evil" (Hebrews 5:14). A scientific statement may seem at first to be evil because it doesn't appear to harmonize with statements in the Bible, whereas further unprejudiced examination may reveal that there is no conflict after all.

HISTORICAL CONFLICTS BETWEEN RELIGION AND SCIENCE

Conflicts between widely held religious beliefs and the theories and discoveries announced by scientists are not new. History is an eloquent source of testimony on this topic. It records events that have taken place and statements that have been made which none of us can change because they are history. Pertinent to the present discussion are many instances of religious scholars strongly proclaiming as dogma their perceptions about what the Bible teaches concerning the Earth and the universe. Their views were later shown to be unnecessarily restrictive ideas. These examples sugggest the use of great caution on the part of Bible teachers today in presenting unnecessarily restrictive meanings of certain scriptures. If they don't want to consider these examples, that is their privilege; they can be like the ostrich. The following paragraphs review reactions of influential religious thinkers during the last eighteen centuries to announcements of scientific theories and discoveries about the structure of our universe. These theories and discoveries were in the field of astronomy, and accounts of them will be found in any current introductory textbook on the subject.

AN EARLY SCIENTFIC THEORY ACCEPTED AS DOGMA

One of the most famous astronomers of antiquity was Claudius Ptolemy, who lived in the second century A.D. He published a summary of previous achievements in astronomy along with some of his own notable contributions. His most significant original contribution was a geometrical representation of the solar system that predicted the apparent locations of the planets with considerable accuracy. He used a very complex model called "the geocentric system," which placed the Earth at the center of things and assumed that the sun and the other planets revolved around the Earth in perfectly circular orbits. The basic geocentric idea did not originate with Ptolemy. It did not describe reality, and Ptolemy made no claim that it did. However, the medieval mind readily accepted authority and absolute dogma, especially when a religious hierarchy took an official stand on a matter that it believed to be within its domain. The geocentric theory held sway in human thought for nearly 1500 years following Ptolemy's day. This is an example of how a theory can be completely wrong and yet win long-term acceptance by those most expert in the field, so long as it is in accord with the observational data available at the time.

It is a curious thing that religionists who delve into things totally out of their field will incorporate into their dogma technical concepts about the natural world that are clearly beyond the purview of the spiritual message they presume to teach. The medieval Church adopted the geocentric theory as part and parcel of its dogma concerning what the Holy Spirit teaches in the Bible.... They seem to have thought it necessary to have a full rigorous technical explanation of Biblical passages that refer to the sun, moon, stars, and Earth. As more truth became available to mankind about the interrelationships of these bodies, it was inevitable that conflicts would arise between the dogmatic position of religious hierarchies and hypotheses put forth by scientists trying to explain the results of their observations of celestial objects.

A MORE ACCURATE VIEW, YET DENOUNCED

Early in the sixteenth century the famous Polish astronomer Nicholas Copernicus came on the scene of history. He was serving as a professor in a church-controlled university in Rome when he announced his theory that the sun and planets do not revolve about the Earth, but that the Earth and other planets revolve about the sun . . . the "heliocentric" concept of the solar system. The new theory was rejected by most of his peers for several years, as "a mere hypothesis." It was so revolutionary that Copernicus moved back to Poland and kept quiet about it for thirty years. Finally he gained the courage to get his ideas into print. His heliocentric theory was set forth in a book published in May, 1543, while he was on his deathbed. The medieval Church reacted with strong opposition. In the universities under the Church's control, the professors were instructed to teach only "safe science," in line with scriptural truth as interpreted by the theological professors.[2]

Martin Luther and John Calvin were contemporaries of Copernicus. Their voices also were given to join the criticism of the heliocentric theory by the medieval Church. Luther spoke derisively:

> People gave ear to an upstart astrologer who strove to show that the earth revolves, not the heavens or the firmament, the sun and the moon. Whoever wishes to appear clever must devise some new system, which of all systems is of course the very best. This fool wishes to reverse the entire science of astronomy; but sacred scripture tells us that Joshua commanded the sun to stand still, and not the earth.[3]

Martin Luther had a scholarly and prominent associate named Philip Melanchthon who also condemned Copernicus. He wrote a treatise entitled "Elements of Physics" in which he stated:

> "The eyes are witnesses that the heavens revolve in the space of twenty-four hours. But certain men, either from the love of novelty, or to make a display of ingenuity, have concluded that the earth moves; and they maintain that neither the eighth sphere nor the sun revolves . . . . Now it is a want of honesty and decency to assert such notions publicly, and the example is pernicious. It is the part of a good mind to accept the truth as revealed by God and to acquiesce in it."

He cited passages in the Psalms and in Ecclesiastes which he claimed showed that the Earth stands still and that the sun moves around the earth.[4]

Without doubt Luther and Melanchthon thought they were defending God's word and true Christian doctrine against the impious teachings of a scientist. It seems that what they were doing wrong was treating the Bible as a technical science book! Rheticus and Reinhold, two capable astronomers who taught at the same university at Wittenberg as Luther, convinced themselves that the heliocentric theory of the solar system was true, but neither was allowed to teach that idea to his students![5]

John Calvin took the lead among other Protestant churches that attacked Copernicus. In his "Commentary on Genesis," Calvin condemned all who asserted that the earth is not at the center of the universe. He thought he clinched the matter by quoting Psalms 93:1, "The world is firmly established; it cannot be moved." He then asked, "Who will venture to place the authority of Copernicus above that of the Holy Spirit?" [6] Does that charge have a familiar ring in the twentieth century? Two hundred years after Calvin another well-known theologian, John Wesley, declared that these new ideas about the earth and other planets going around the sun "tend toward infidelity." [7]

SUPPORTING OBSERVATIONS INCREASE THE OPPOSITION

Galileo was a famous Italian astronomer who had exceptional ability as a mathematician and experimenter. It is reported that as a student he incurred the wrath of his professors by refusing to accept on faith dogmatic statements based solely on the authority of great writers of the past. In the last decade of the sixteenth century he publicly announced that he had adopted the Copernican hypothesis of the solar system, which certainly was not a popular philosophy among medieval Church circles in Italy, where he taught at the University of Padua. The attack of theologians came against Galileo with great force. The first instance was in 1610, when he announced that his crude telescope had revealed the moons of the planet Jupiter.

Galileo's theologian-adversaries recognized that this development took the Copernican theory out of the realm of hypothesis. The discovery of moons orbiting around Jupiter increased the number of known planetary bodies in our solar system (including our moon) beyond the count of seven. They proceeded to denounce both his method and its results as absurd and impious. Quoting the Bible, they claimed the seven golden candlesticks of the Apocalypse, the seven-branched candlestick of the tabernacle, and the seven churches of Asia were "types" which PROVED there could be only seven planets.[8] Their confident but foolish misapplication of scripture was premature; the eighth major planet, Uranus, was dicovered in 1781. Neptune was seen in 1846, and Pluto was discovered in 1930.

Galileo's telescope was kept busy. Historians record that opponents of Copernicus had told him, "If your doctrine were true, Venus would show phases like the moon," whereupon Copernicus responded, "You are right; I know not what to say; but God is good, and will in time find an answer to this objection." Whether in fulfillment of this prophecy of Copernicus or not, the answer came in 1611, when the phases of the planet Venus were seen through Galileo's telescope. I would suggest that Satan did not lead Galileo to make that discovery, and, that Galileo was not seeking to discredit the Holy Scriptures in any way.

Much has been written about Galileo's struggle, his persecution by the Church, and its vain attempts to show by the Scriptures that his scientifically discovered "truths" were just not true. Like those who attacked Copernicus, they were zealous in misusing the Bible as a technical science book to support preconceived notions about what the Scriptures taught. They were extremely dogmatic concerning what the Holy Spirit said in Scripture about technical aspects of the natural world, a topic which had nothing to do with the spiritual message of the Bible. Furthermore, they were commenting on Biblical passages which did not even contain such explicit details.

In 1873 the publishing house of the Lutheran Synod of Missouri, published a book with the German title, *Astronomische Unterredung* (Astronomical Discussion), in which he stated, "the entire Holy Scripture settles the question that the Earth is the principal body of the universe, that it stands fixed, and the sun and moon only serve to light it."[10] That happened long after Johannes Kepler and Sir Isaac Newton had firmly demonstrated the laws of gravitation and orbital motion which are at work in the solar system, and which are relied upon extensively in space exploration programs today.

DETECTING THE EXPANSION OF THE OBSERVABLE UNIVERSE

Skipping ahead to the twentieth century, we find Edwin Hubble using the 100-inch telescope on Mt. Wilson in California to make extensive studies in 1923 and 1924 of the structure of our system of stars. He used measurements of the shifts in the wave length of light emanating from recognized, "standard" stars to show that the farther away they are, the faster they are receding from the Earth's location. He showed that many patches of stars believed earlier to be a part of our Milky Way galaxy were in reality separate galaxies, situated thousands of light years away. His exciting results were announced at the winter meeting of the American Astronomical Society in 1924. The relation between the distances and the velocity of recession of these remote star systems came to be known as Hubble's Law.

Thrilling as these findings were, many scientists, including Albert Einstein, were reluctant to accept them, because they implied that the universe had a beginning point . . . an instant of creation. They further implied that all matter and energy in the universe must have been concentrated in a primordial atom which exploded in a cosmic fireball of unimaginable intensity . . . an explosion the remnants of which might still be seen receding into the outer reaches of space.

This is, of course, the "Big Bang " theory of the universe, which contrasts sharply with the "Steady State" theory. Key elements in interpreting Hubble's data were: the velocity of light, a universal constant which had been repeatedly measured since 1676; and the Doppler Effect, which explains the apparent shift in frequency and wave length of a light wave when the source of that wave is moving away from the observer. An inseparable part of the conclusions from these results is that the light from remote galaxies began its journey toward us thousands, millions, and in some cases billions of years ago. That is indeed a conclusion in which high confidence can be placed, because the basic principle is demonstrated every time a spacecraft sends us observational data via radio waves over a known path length from the outer planets of the solar system.

The data just reviewed has driven scientists to the conclusion that the universe must have an age between fifteen and twenty billion years. It should be pointed out that *the dedicated scientists who made these discoveries were not trying to find proof that the earth has existed for a long period of time in order to support Darwin's theory of biological evolution!* Their scientific pursuits were in no way related to studies of organic evolution. From research in the fields of physics and astronomy they discovered strong evidences that we have a very old universe of which the sun and its nine planets form a very minuscule part. The Big Bang theory should be viewed as a totally separate concept from the theory of organic evolution. The two should not be confused. Anyone who thinks that all scientists who accept the data indicating a very old universe automatically believe in "amoeba-to-man" biological evolution is grievously misinformed. The evidence which demonstrates the age of the universe to be several billion years stands totally independent of geological and paleontological studies of the earth's crust. Furthermore, the theories about spontaneous generation of life and organic evolution were developed independently from the astronomical research which revealed to mankind that the universe was formed billions of years ago.

Scientists are subjective human beings like everyone else, and are reluctant to recant a long-held theory which they have spent much time and effort to substantiate. Albert Einstein published his Theory of General Relativity in 1917, and didn't realize that his equations inherently predicted an expanding universe, a concept in conflict with his belief in a Steady-State universe. Even after Hubble's announcement in 1924 of the physical evidence of an expanding universe of galaxies, Einstein, like many other astronomers, held on to the Steady-State theory. Six years later, however, he traveled to Mt. Wilson and saw the evidence himself through Hubble's 100-inch telescope. In later years he admitted full acceptance of the idea of "a beginning."

In relatively recent history substantial new evidence was accidentally discovered which greatly tipped the scales in astronomical circles in favor of the Big Bang theory. That was the recording in 1965 by Arno Penzias and Robert Wilson of radio-wavelength thermal radiation arriving from all directions in the universe. The radiation they detected corresponded exactly to what George Gamow had predicted in 1948 that should be observable from the remnant of the original creation "fireball," long delayed in reaching the Earth and greatly extended in wavelength because it originated at such a great distance, estimated to be between 15 and 20 billion light years. This is not to imply that their measurement confirmed the full Genesis account of the creation; it merely provided additional credibility to the theory set forth by Edwin Hubble and others that the universe is very old and has been expanding since the instant of its creation.

REACTIONS OF TWENTIETH CENTURY THEOLOGIANS

What are the reactions of theologians of our day to the new data God has allowed man to measure about the vastness of His universe and of its apparent great age? Many of them have of course welcomed information which lends support to the Genesis statement about creation of "the heavens and the earth" at a given point in history — the Beginning.[11] And they also are pleased with the tentative conclusions of scientists that the universe was created out of nothing. No physical laws or evidence have yet been set forth which explain the source of the incredible amounts of matter and energy which must have been released in the primeval fireball.

However, many writers do not like the discovery of evidence purporting to show that the universe (including the Earth) just might possibly be older than 6,000 years. One example is that of Henry M. Morris, a former civil engineering professor who, though he reportedly had no formal theological training, has written a great deal on religious subjects. In 1976 Morris published a 716 page commentary of the book of Genesis called "The Genesis Record." He has been characterized as "a creation scientist." He has written much good material, but he is often quoted as "a scientific authority" by well-meaning people, even when he discusses concepts that are outside his technical field.

For example, one of Morris' ideas occasionally quoted is a comment about the starlight impinging on the Earth during the creation "days" of Genesis, and the dilemma created by modern measured data showing that light from the more distant stars has taken billions of years to reach the Earth. He states:

> It therefore did not take a billion years for the light from a star which is a billion light-years distant from the Earth after the star was created. The light-trail from the star was created in transit, as it were, all the

way from the star to the Earth, three days before the star itself was created![12]

That is indeed imaginative maneuvering in a vain attempt to explain away something which exists (the data showing a transit time of billions of years for starlight to reach the Earth) in order to protect a cherished and unnecessarily restrictive impression about the chronology of creation events related in the Genesis account. It is an example of the "ostrich effect." It is most certainly the privilege of anyone to hypothesize and even believe such an explanation about a star's light being released before the star is created, but no one has the right to insist or imply that others should believe that God's word teaches such.

In the teaching of astronomy one important task is explaining the observed changes which take place in stars. There are extensive data on variation in light output, spectral characteristics, and dimensions of many stars over the days, months, years, and centuries. The stars actually do change with time. The explanation of why and how they change uses a mixture of theory and data. Extensive measurements have been conducted over the last decade by observatories in Hawaii and Arizona of nineteen "red giant" stars which exhibit substantial variations in their infrared radiation and their cyclic periods of variation have been determined. These stars are believed by astronomers to be in the latter stages of their life cycle. Whether that theory is true or not, it has been an established fact for over half a century that such stars vary noticeably in their intensity in a cyclic fashion.

The notion that stars change their characteristics with time is well beyond the hypothesis stage. Astronomers label the general topic of changes that take place in stars over time "stellar evolution." This may come across as a provocative title to students who have been conditioned to suspect the use of the word "evolution," whether in politics, biology, art, or astronomy. Some stars (the supernovae) which were observed in centuries past to have sudden thousand-fold and higher increases in light output for a few days left luminous expanding gas clouds which are regularly measured by astronomers to track their speeds of expansion through the years. Because of dedicated observations, additonal supernovae events and remnants continue to be identified.

In his Genesis commentary, Henry Morris reacted as follows to the data on supernova measurements:

> As noted earlier, the universe was created "full-grown" from the beginning; God did not require millions of years to develop it into its intended usable form. The purpose of the heavenly bodies was 'to give light upon the earth;' so this is what they did, right from the beginning. Some have objected to this concept on the basis of revolutionary changes supposedly taking place in the stars. The fact is, however, no one has ever observed such changes taking place. As long as men have been observing the stars, they have always looked as they do now, The only possible exception of any consequence to this statement might be the novas or supernovas that are occasionally observed in the heavens that apparently heat up or explode, and that some of them have been observed in galaxies supposedly hundreds of thousands of light-years from the earth; the argument is, therefore, that the stellar event producing the nova or supernova must have taken place the corresponding number of hundreds of thousands of years ago. This might constitute a minor problem.[13]

In attempting to develop possible answers to this "minor problem," Morris proceeded to assail the validity of astronomers' methods of estimating distances to these remote objects, and to claim that there are respectable models of physics which yield light motions allowing light to reach the earth from INFINITE distances in "only a few years." Such a statement contradicts physical laws established by the Creator which he has allowed mankind to discover and utilize. As a last alternative he stated that there is no reason why God could not have created "pulses" in the beginning, which when they reach the Earth would be interpreted as, say, novas, when they were in reality merely created "bursts" of energy in the light trails connecting with various stars.[14]

With all due respect, the latter is obviously a fanciful notion, and Morris admitted that the reason for God doing such a thing is not yet clear. Such a notion is essentially analogous to suggesting that the planet Mars does not really exist, but the illusion that there is a planet in that orbit is caused by varying intensities of continuously created light pulses which happen to have the special characteristics of sunlight reflected from reddish soil, to make it appear that another planet is actually out there in space.

The purpose of relating the above excerpts from *The Genesis Record* commentary is to illustrate the foolishness of trying to explain away carefully measured scientific data about the universe in order to minimize its conflict with restrictive interpretations of the Genesis creation account. Most enlightened students will not accept such explanations, and it is unwise to pressure them into it.

IMPLICATIONS FOR CHRISTIAN TEACHERS OF SCIENCE

How does all this affect a Christian engaged in teaching the science of astronomy? One area is in the selection of new textbooks every few years to keep up with the rapid pace of discoveries in astronomy; we want the students to have the most up-to-date information possible. However, in typical textbooks they will meet head-on with a blended menu of unproven hypotheses (sometimes clothed as facts) and theories whose dependability has been demonstrated repeatedly by physical measurements. For the last few years many of the newer texts in introductory astronomy have included a chapter or an "epilogue" presenting the supposed accidental beginning of life upon the Earth, followed by an outline of amoeba-to-man evolution. In some cases it is tied in with the description of efforts being made to detect the existence of life elsewhere in the universe . . . "listening" for radio signals from a planet circling some distant star, or searching for evidence of organic life forms on the planet Mars. Apparently the motivation for such efforts lies in the "assumption" that life began accidentally on planet Earth, a theory unsupported by evidence, and one which a science teacher can openly reject as unproved. When an instructor knows that an unproven theory is being represented as a fact in a textbook, it is academic dishonesty not to call that to the attention of the class.

By careful screening, one can find some of the newer astronomy textbooks in which the organic evolution theory is minimized; it may be present but not pervasive. A few authors have the wisdom to state that astronomers have no business trying to define what constitutes "life." A textbook should be selected which has high credibility in its field, and in order to select an astronomy text which includes the new data acquired by x-ray, visible light, and infrared telescopes in space, as well as by the ground-based radio telescopes, a teacher must usually accept a book which has material presenting the theory that life forms began accidentally on our planet. And in some cases the authors do not bother with labeling it as a theory. It is skillfully presented propaganda for a totally mechanistic view of the universe and the origin of life. Such material is really out of place in an astronomy text. If it is found there it can be skipped or identified for what it is. The best situation is where Christian students have skilled Christian teachers, who can guide them in the proper use of their text.

Another way the potential conflict between science and religious views affects us as Christian teachers of science is in our choosing the stance taken in the classroom on these issues. With kindness and respect for the dignity of the individual, students should be allowed to retain any restricted view they may have of such things as the age of the universe. However, they need to become familiar with the expanding universe model, the data supporting it, and the fact that many scientists and others with whom they may work believe in a very old age

for the universe and Earth, IRRESPECTIVE OF ANY BE-
LIEF IN DARWINIAN EVOLUTION. We are obliged to
help them comprehend all the amazing and beautiful things
about the universe mankind has been allowed to discover,
being careful to distinguish between untested hypotheses and
those theories deserving some credibility because they are
undergirded with impressive measured data. For example, a
properly taught astronomy course will not include any material
which will contradict the teaching of Genesis that Adam was
specially created from the elements of the earth God had previously brought into existence.

Christian teachers of science need to impart the knowledge,
theories, and vocabulary of science with candor and fairness
without failing to make known their personal belief in the
Creator of all things. When a theory which is clearly unfounded
and anti-Biblical is set forth in a text students should be ap-
prised of the dubious nature of such material. They should be
taught to discern between "hard data" and theoretical concepts
dreamed up by the mind of man. Astronomy students can be
reassured that the non-scientific (but true) Genesis account of
the origin of the universe does not place a limit on how far
back in time its creation occurred, and that the evidence God
has allowed man to discover in the twentieth century indicating
that the universe had a definite beginning point is generally
supportive of the statements in Genesis that it had a beginning
and that it was created. This general agreement has been
realized by many leading astronomers of our day, even some
who are avowed agnostics.

It should be remembered that the astronomical evidence
strongly indicating that the universe had a beginning point and
has existed for billions of years neither confirms nor contradicts
those brief statements in Genesis about the sequence and
identity of created life forms. To quote a highly respected
researcher and educator in the field of astronomy, the late
George Abell:

> Science neither confirms nor refutes the Genesis story of the creation. Science is concerned with an interpretation of nature — not an explanation. Science begins with observations, or the results of experiments, and attempts to find a model (or hypothesis, or theory) that predicts those — and other — observations and experimental results as consequences of that model's basic postulates. A scientific hypothesis, however, can never claim to be absolutely true, because ultimately every absolute truth must be based on premises of faith — a subject science does not, and cannot — deal with.[15]

Abell's statement sounds like science can be taught from a completely neutral standpoint. Unfortunately human nature makes that nigh to impossible. Just as facial expressions, tone of voice, and relative emphasis on words by a television commentator can "telegraph" his or her editorial opinion on news items, the teacher in a classroom can effectively influence the students with a particular personal viewpoint regarding the meaning or validity of a theory. It is well known that an atheist who teaches science (or any other subject) can use that position to propagate atheism — particularly if the textbook material is conveniently aligned with his viewpoint. Textbooks, however valid they may be in reporting data, can be very arbitrary and biased in the interpretation of that data, because they are written by subjective human beings. To offset this tendency, a Christian teacher must make a conscious effort to point out where the textbook material is flawed, questionable, unfounded or totally inaccurate where atheistic statements are made.

These conclusions have been reached specifically about how to deal with the challenges of teaching astronomy from a Christian perspective, with the teachers handling in a responsible way their knowledge of what is truth and what is theory, regardless of what the science textbook may say. Some of the ideas may be applicable to teaching in the life sciences such as biology. There the task is undoubtedly far more difficult, because students must be taught what the general organic evolution theory is and become familiar with a vocabulary which tacitly assumes it is true, since the theory that life on this planet began accidentally and that human beings merely represent the end product of a long series of evolutionary steps is strongly embedded in the structure of teaching and research in the biological sciences.

IMPLICATIONS FOR BIBLE TEACHERS

It has been pointed out from history that centuries before Charles Darwin and his theory of organic evolution came on the scene, both Catholic and Protestant theologians were far too dogmatic in making pronouncements about the arrangement of the sun and planets in our solar system, citing Biblical passages as support for their position. They may have done so in all innocence and with good intent, but they were dealing with a technical issue unrelated to the Christian gospel, and beyond the legitimate bounds of Bible teaching. In a similar way, Bible teachers of today are sometimes prone to be too dogmatic about what the Bible says about the age of the Earth, as part of a sincere attempt to refute Darwin's theories. People today have a perfect right to believe that the earth is only 6,000 years old, just as Martin Luther, John Calvin, and John Wesley had a right to believe that the sun revolves around the earth. However, since such beliefs cannot be substantiated with technical certainty from the scriptures and are not even a part of the spiritual message of the Bible, they should not be lumped in as a tenet of Christian belief necessary to be pleasing to God.

An on-going debate rages about the validity of the "molecules-to-man" theory of evolution. There appears to be an adequate number of qualified Christian geneticists, biologists, and anthropologists capable of showing that such a theory must be forever relegated to the category of an unsubstantiated hypothesis. Bible teachers can confidently speak of the special creation of man from the dust (elements) of the Earth as mentioned in Genesis because we believe it to be revealed truth. It is a truth which cannot be disproved by scientists though there are many emotional claims made to the contrary. What can Bible teachers say about the creation events which occurred prior to man's creation? Following the first two verses of Genesis, the preparation of man's habitat and the creation of birds, fish, and land animals can be related just as they are presented in Scripture without being any more detailed and specific than the Biblical passages permit. It is the best policy to be neutral about what we can infer from the Bible alone concerning the age of the Earth and the time-duration of the segments of the creation, since the Biblical account is appropriately lacking in scientific and technical detail. This is especially important when teaching teenagers through adults. Remember that God allowed Galileo to observe details about the solar system he made, and his observations showed that the theologians of his day were unwise (and in error) in proclaiming dogmatic views about the solar system, claiming they were based firmly on Biblical truth. Most educated teenagers and adults today have learned of the data mankind has acquired revealing billion-year old starlight just now reaching the planet earth. We will lose our credibility as Bible teachers if we ignore that reality. It will do no good to behave like the ostrich in such a situation.

If one believes in the God of the Bible, we certainly cannot limit what He can do. One should not "force fit" his or her own ideas into the brief, beautiful, pristine creation account in Genesis and insist that all others interpret it as "clear Biblical testimony" that the creation of the universe occurred only 6,000 years ago. Such information is simply not present in Genesis. This does not deny that the Genesis record is a "historical account." A record does not have to be highly specific and technically in depth to be accepted as a true record. The central theme has nothing directly to do with the sciences of astronomy, geology, or biology, even though the record refers to some objects which man selected centuries later as the subject matter for those sciences.

NOTES

1. Trout, Virgil R., "Christianity And Science," in *20th Century Christian*, December 1967, p. 10. (Permission to quote given verbally by Virgil Trout).

2. White, Andrew D., *A History of the Warfare of Science With Theology in Christendom*, Vol. I, Dover Publications, 1960 Reprint, p.126. (Book now out of print).

3. Ibid.

4. Ibid.

5. Ibid, p. 129.

6. Ibid, p. 127.

7. Ibid, p. 128.

8. Ibid, p. 131.

9. Ibid, p. 130.

10. Ibid, p. 150.

11. Jastrow, Robert, *God and the Astronomers*, W.W. Norton & Co., 1978, p. 16.

12. Morris, Henry M., *The Genesis Record*, Baker Book House and Creation-Life Publishers, San Diego, 1976, p. 65. (Letter sent 8/23/87 requesting permission to quote).

13. Ibid, p. 66.

14. Ibid.

15. Abell, George O., *Drama of the Universe*, Holt, Rinehart and Winston, 1973, p. 1. (Letter sent 8/23/87 requesting permission to quote).

9

GENERAL OBSERVATIONS

J. D. T H O M A S

W e now consider the first twelve "Problems for This Study" listed in Chapter I, Introduction, since these pertain to the fields of Philosophy and Science. Number thirteen will be discussed later in Section IV, where we will be discussing the Bible and its teaching. In this section we repeat, for purposes of emphasis, some of the ideas set forth by the previous authors. We discuss the problems by number:

1. *Definitions.* So many people use the term "evolution" vaguely. They do not realize that the theory of evolution which is opposed by Christians ("creationists") is "evolution from scratch on up," or as sometimes said, from "amoeba to man," and in which there is a denial of the existence of God and of creation. On the other hand, there are changes in the structure of organisms at the lower levels of the taxa (species and genera), which many people call "evolution." At this level such changes do "evolve," from one form into some other closely related form as time passes. No doubt teachers sometimes use the term "evolution" when all they intend to communicate is "such changes, or variations, or speciation (as discussed quite thoroughly by Dr.Nichols in chapter 4)." Such terminology,

however, sends up a "red flag" to some other person who may think only of "amoeba to man" and a "denial of creation" when he hears the word evolution.

Macro-evolution is the technical term often used now to mean the "amoeba to man" view. It literally means "Big Evolution." It holds that *all forms of life on earth originally came from one or a very few primitive life-forms by a conneccted series of changes, which at every point were controlled only by nature.* Julian S.Huxley, world famous evolution advocate, has said, "all reality is a single process of evolution."[1]

The term for minor evolution, meaning only variations of a minimum type, up to and including speciation, is Micro-evolution. The micro-evolution changes are brought about by mutations, recombinations, and natural selection, as Dr. Nichols has shown in Chapter 4. J.N.Moore, arguing against a radical evolutionary point of view, has stated that these "are sources only of differences of characteristic expressions of traits already in existence, and not a source of new traits."[2]

2. *The Authority of Science.* The domain of science, since it is dependent upon observation, is the physical, material world of solids, liquids and gases. It can deal only with those realities that can be weighed, measured, touched, numbered and divided. Science is "out of bounds" as far as metaphysical realities such as values, spiritual realities, and abstract entities are concerned. It cannot deal with love, beauty, loyalty, courage, goodness and such like, but these things are very real, and true and false statements can be made about them. So there are two realms of reality — that of physical things that science can deal with, and that of mental or spiritual things — e.g., values — which science cannot deal with. It is very important to realize that science truly is limited to things it can observe, weigh, measure, touch, divide, and other similar sensed observations, and that it has no authority beyond what it can actually prove. Science "doesn't know everything!"

For anyone to claim that there is no reality that science is not an authority about, is to be guilty of "Scientism," the philosophy that makes of science a sort of a "sacred cow," able to know everything. Religion has no quarrel with strict science or true science; but it feels free to oppose some "loose science" ideas or concepts which are sometimes claimed to be scientific but which are based only upon inferences or perhaps wishful thinking. Some inferences can be valid, of course, but they are not to be counted as *fact*, since they cannot be demonstrated to be true.

It is impossible for science to say whether there be a God or not, or whether he created the world, whether man is a spirit being, or whether adultery is immoral. These are not determinable by scientific observation, and therefore are out of bounds to science. Science can handle quantities but not qualities. Langdon B. Gilkey has aptly stated:

> "...to rule out God's activity because it cannot become a part of a scientific explanation of events, is to draw a philosophical conclusion which is not itself a part of a scientific hypothesis. The naturalistic world view is an extension of a scientific understanding beyond the range of science."[3]

We call attention again to Dr. Hoover's distinction between "strict science" and "loose science" (Chapter 2). Strict science is real science, where the conclusions are based upon actual observation, upon five-sense (empirical) knowledge, something that can be repeated and/or demonstrated. In strict science *facts* are determined. But in loose science there can be no observation, no demonstrable knowledge, no facts, but only inferences, extrapolations, and perhaps wishful thinking. Since Macro-evolution is not repeatable and cannot be observed, it can only be a conclusion of loose science and cannot be called a "fact."

There is no known scientific mechanism for Macro-evolution. On the other hand, micro-evolution (such as speciation) changes are demonstrable by strict science and the mechanisms that produce them are known. This is why the Christian accepts the possibility of certain micro-evolution changes in organisms but rejects Macro-evolution. He accepts strict science but does not necessarily accept certain inferences of loose science. With true science, based on hard facts, he can still believe in God, in the Bible and in creation.

3. *The Age of the Earth and the Universe.* In chapter 7 Dr. Sadler pointed out some of the scientific reasons why many people believe the earth and the universe are "of great age," as versus the doctrine of "a young earth," held by some creationists. We list here some of his conclusions, for the sake of further emphasis:

A. *The radioactive dating "clocks,"* themselves scientific facts, have apparently been disintegrating for eons. The carbon 14 (14C) method of dating is the best known of these. Other elements are used, however, in dating the earth, the galaxy, and the universe since they have a much longer half-life.

B. *The expanding universe and the big bang.* The expanding universe is a demonstrable scientific fact, and if the assumption is correct that its rate has been constant, then there was a time when the universe was all together in a small space. This also fits the creation view.

C. *The Second Law of Thermodynamics.* This law declares that "the universe is running down," that is, energy flows from hot to cold, or from highly ordered states to disordered states (example: Uranium turning into lead). There had to be a beginning, or creation, since if the universe has always existed, all the energy would by now have become disordered, or would have arrived at "heat death," where life would no longer be sustained.

D. *A young universe and earth with the appearance of age.* If the earth were only a few thousand years old (say 10,000 or less), many of its features would have an artificial appearance of great age — such as trees with many annual rings; nuclei appearing to have decayed from unstable parent nuclei; expanding galaxies; annual layers on the polar ice caps; light rays appearing to be from distant galaxies but created in flight, without having originated from the galaxies at all, which really hadn't been created yet. Light travels at 186,000 miles per second, and a "light year" is the distance it travels in one year. For light to be travelling from a distant galaxy for millions of light years, indicates that the galaxy had been up there longer than a few thousand years.

The problem here is that although Adam and Eve were no doubt created as adults rather than as newly born infants, in their case it was required in order for them to be able to cope with life, but there seems to be no reason why all the other factors needed to have been created so recently, with the appearance of age (e.g., starlight created 'in flight' on its way to the earth before the star itself was created). Of course God could have done such things. He has adequate power to do whatever he sees fit. In fact, he could have created the entire universe and all of us in it last night at twelve o'clock, with us having "built-in memories" of all that we now believe happened to us in the past. He has the power to have done all these things, but we have no logical reason why he would have done it this way, and, as we shall see in the Bible section later, such a faith in a "young earth" is not required in order to have a valid Christian faith. Our point is, that the earth can be either "young," or "old," without interfering with Christian faith. The question cannot be settled on absolute, strict science basis. One can be fully Christian without worrying about this problem. It is a non-issue. As to the recency of man, we shall comment later on this.

4. *Uniformitarianism vs. Catastrophism.* In Chapter 3 Dr. Felix has furnished a very thorough discussion of Uniformitarianism and Catastrophism. Uniformitarianism, the "cornerstone of geology," is necessarily "loose science" since it is based upon the assumption that "the present is the key to the past," and the processes that bring about events have always been the same without any change. Nature does act with some uniformity but there certainly have been some catastrophes, as Dr. Felix has shown, and these are not explained nor integrated very well into the total outlook of the average uniformitarian geologist.

The Geologic Time-table is also an artificial construct, being based upon uniformitarian theory, and cannot, therefore, be counted as having an absolute factual basis, although it no doubt has some relative values. It has real possibilities for weakness in dating, since there is no one place on earth where there is a complete geological record, and huge assumptions have been made where there is no strict-science evidence.

The known catastrophes of the past rightly call for consideration as to date and impact. The huge fossil "graveyards," the frozen forests of the Arctic, the frozen mammal deposits in Siberia, the Ice Age evidence, the geological evidence of Plate Tectonics, and indeed the Biblical flood, all indicate that powerful catastrophes have happened suddenly and were not the result of ordinary "uniformitarian" influences. Of course it cannot be proved that catastrophes explain all the actual rock and other geological formations that exist, but they must certainly be part of the overall true explanation.

Probably the most we can say about geology and its potential for dating, is that at present we do not have enough information to be positive and final in our conclusions. It is impossible, therefore, to operate on a strict science basis, and so we must leave this area open-ended, at least for now. There is not a single, absolute fact known, however, that would contradict faith in God, faith in the Bible, or faith in the creation. These are all intellectually respectable, since all challenges to them are in the realm of loose science.

5. *The Flood.* There is at present no scientific evidence that the Flood of Genesis 6-8 actually occurred, nor is there any such evidence that it did not occur. For several years, there have been numerous efforts to find the remains of Noah's ark on Mount Ararat, but today theories for or against the flood are still in the realm of faith. The faith of the naturalistic view assumes that the Genesis flood account is fictional, and that it is only one of numerous flood accounts in the various cultures of ancient times. The Gilgamesh Epic is the most elaborate account found among the pagan materials, and critical scholars

have given much effort to try to show parallels between it and the Genesis account and to claim "Hebrew borrowing" in the production of the Genesis account. The *differences* between the various ancient flood accounts are far more significant than the similarities, however, the Hebrew version being much more refined and reasonable. Probably each of the several versions were handed down from the actual historical event, the Hebrew account being refined and accurate due to inspiration.

There is a great debate about whether the flood was geographically local or universal in scope, and if only local, whether it was anthropologically universal or local. There are strong arguments for each of the various conclusions,[4] but there are still many unanswered questions: the age of the earth; the possible date of the flood; the collection and distribution of animals before and after the flood; the distribution of humans after the flood, and other matters. These problems are not unsolvable, but they have not been clearly worked out yet.

Both the uniformitarians and the "young earth" people have problems. The chief problem for uniformitarians is still the original *assumption* of the fact of uniformitarian philosophy. There is no way to be certain that change has always been constant, and that there have been no significant catastrophes, so the philosophy of uniformitarianism must always remain in the "loose science" realm. The "young earth" adherents also have serious problems: e.g., the date of the flood; and whether the one flood could have produced all the present geological formations which seem to have different ages. Suffice it to say that either group could be right, at least in their major views, but since questions about the flood cannot today be settled by strict science methods, we should realize that the issues *need not be settled* in order for a person to have a valid Christian faith. Both of the present conclusions are faith conclusions!

6. *Paleontology.* It is generally agreed that the real proof of evolution has to be based upon the fossil finds. There have been "artistic constructs" in the major museums showing how man has evolved, and how horses have evolved up to their

present form. We must keep in mind that these are only artificial constructions, based upon imagination and prepared to fit a preconceived evolutionary theory. There is no connected series of fossils found in any one location on the earth that can illustrate evolution! The fossil remains that might be used to illustrate evolution are found in locations different from each other and thus there is no evidence of their descent from one another or relation to each other.

Again, a big problem for evolutionists is that when fossils appear they are fully developed into modern forms — there are no "transition fossils" — and they appear abruptly, with no indication of their origin or relation to previous organisms. An excellent illustration of this is in the Cambrian, or first fossil deposits. Many separate, fully formed organisms appeared there suddenly. Later, new forms appeared suddenly, fully developed, with no indication of gradual evolution, as Darwinism claims.[5] If macro-evolution were really true, there would be all manner of in-between or transitional fossils, because Darwin claimed that evolution was slow and gradual. The great gaps in the fossil record has proved to be a great embarassment to those who argue for Darwin's slow, gradual evolution. As a matter of fact it is now admitted that the sudden appearance of new forms in the fossil record shows that evolution was not slow, but occurred in sudden spurts, with stable forms lasting for some time. This has been called "emergent evolution," and "punctuated equilibrium." It will be discussed later.

7. *The Beginning of Life.* Evolutionists hold that the first life came from non-life by natural methods — often called "spontaneous generation." This theory was adopted in order to deny a need for a Creator God and to justify a totally naturalistic, basic worldview. Surprisingly, it denies all scientific knowledge, however, since all that science has observed is that life comes from life. Many efforts have been made to produce life from non-life, but so far to no avail. Organic molecules have been produced in a laboratory, but of course they had no life.

Early theories about spontaneous generation were exploded by Louis Pasteur, who earned fame by showing that microorganisms could not be spontaneously produced in sterile media but were carried in the air, as "germs." Later efforts to prove spontaneous generation are proved fruitless by Dr. Reeves in Chapter 6, by the fact that there are too many amino acids, the nature of proteins is too complex, and, with other factors considered it is simply an impossibility for random, "chance" combinations to produce life. Further, the Genetic Code is too sensitive to hope for the quality of life forms such as we have to have been formed accidentally. To move one gene out of sequence on a chromosome will produce a different organism or a serious distortion of some sort.

Again, we would note that what might have happened in an early earth situation has nothing to do with what might happen in a modern laboratory, where minds are at work in highly controlled situations. Even if life could someday be produced in a test tube, that would not mean that the same thing is what happened without a scientist and without a laboratory in the early earth situation.

Another tremendous problem that evolutionists face, even if spontaneous generation had produced the first gene, or molecule, is that of the gap that would be from that up to the first fossil forms of life that occur in the late Precambrian period. As much evolution would be needed from the first spark of life up to the first one-celled protozoa as it would require to go from there on up to man, according to G.G.Simpson, famed American evolutionist, and, it would be even more complex than the latter span. It is therefore easy to see that faith in evolution is just that, faith and nothing else. It is not scientific.

As far as is known, many advanced life-forms appeared suddenly about the same time in the late Precambrian, fully developed, and they have continued on into the present time without change. They had no ancestors, according to the fossil deposits, so there is a wide gap between them and any first life gene or molecule, if evolution be the way it all happened. This gap has to be filled in by faith, or guessing, since there is no evidence whatever. No scientific observation is possible earlier than those Precambrian, fully developed organisms of which we have fossil remains, therefore, any conclusion concerning life earlier than the fossil record is based on faith and not on factual science.

8. *Taxonomy.* In the Introduction chapter we made mention of the normally accepted list or arrangement of taxa — the scientific groupings of animals. The major division was phyla, with taxonomists varying in opinion from ten to about thirty as the correct number. Each phylum then is composed of several Classes, each class of several Orders, each order of several Families, each family of several Genera, and each genus of several Species. The number in each several division increases greatly, so that when we get to the species classification we are told that there are a million or more separate species. There are many variations within a given species, e.g., within a species of dogs we will have color and many other types of variations.

The question about all of this for evolution-study concerns the Genesis 1 statements about "kinds" of creatures that God made, and which Adam named, as Genesis 2 indicates. From Genesis we get the idea that the kinds of creatures are "fixed," and so we would not expect evolution or any other great changes. From actual experience, however, we have changes at the species level and possibly the genus level. But there are no changes at the phyla level or the classes or orders levels, etc., where there are really major differences between the creatures. Evolutionists wish for the "kinds" of scripture to mean "species," where changes are known, but creationists say that the "kinds" of Genesis refers to the major taxonomic groupings where there is a definite fixity. Again, our present certain knowledge cannot settle this problem, so the conclusion must be left to faith. Either view is a possibility, but it obviously cannot be said that faith in the Bible and in creation is not intellectually respectable, simply because it is "unscientific." Scientists themselves have to exercise great faith at numerous points in their thinking.

9. *The Problem of a Mechanism.* Christian faith in the creation is plausible because it has a mechanism, namely God, as Dr. Felix has observed. God could have caused the existence of all things, because he is omnipotent, as Christians believe. Those who believe in Macro-evolution, however, have a real problem, because they have no mechanism, no Cause that could bring evolution about. They are left to mere "chance" interactions of matter as influenced by the laws of nature. This wonderfully organized universe, with every part so well interrelated (such as the human body) was not planned but just happened, by trial and error, as chance could allow. Even Julian S. Huxley admits the improbability of this:

> Of course, this could not really happen, but it is a useful way of visualizing the fantastic odds against getting a number of favorable mutations in one strain through pure chance alone. A thousand to the millionth power, when written out, becomes the figure 1 with three million noughts after it; and that would take three large volumes of about five hundred pages each, just to print! Actually this is a meaninglessly large figure, but it shows what a degree of improbability natural selection has to surmount, and can circumvent. One with three million noughts after it is the measure of the unlikeliness of a horse — the odds against it happening at all. No one would bet on anything so improbable happening; and yet it has happened. It has happened, thanks to the working of natural selection and the properties of living substance which make natural selection possible.[6]

Huxley's astounding statement is contrary to all the common sense that any of us can muster. It is so improbable that "it could not really happen," so to accept evolution by chance is to have a FAITH — one that is harder to conceive than to believe in God's creative activity.

We remember that a mechanism for Micro-evolution, or minor changes, has been determined, and is real and acceptable. (See Dr. Nichol's discussion in Chapter 4). What evolutionists do at this point therefore is to take what is true for Micro-evolution and *extrapolate* it to Macro-evolution. The word 'extrapolate' means "to conjecture that data which fits a known area applies equally well in an unknown area." So the evolutionists would extrapolate the mechanism which works in

Micro-evolution, to Macro-evolution, by *assuming* that the same mechanism works also for the major groupings of the taxa. The trouble with doing this is that there is no evidence whatever that the mechanism will work or has worked in these major divisions of life-forms. The mechanism *can be demonstrated* and observed for the species category, but there is no scientific evidence of any kind that any organism in one phylum ever had an ancestor in another phylum — that the butterfly and the elephant, for example, have common ancestors (or even men and frogs). *Sometimes* extrapolating can be justifiable, such as in predicting the weather from a familiar cloud-formation, but to believe that "all reality is a single process of evolution," requires more credulity than it does to believe that a loving heavenly Father has created the universe and made man in his own image for his own purposes.

10. *The Antiquity of Man.* Compared with the age of the universe and the age of the earth, the coming of man upon the earth is *very recent*, according to everybody's thinking. Evolutionists would have man to be a few million years old, since they need much time for his development, while creationists, on the other hand, believe that man's arrival was only a few thousand years ago. Creationists accept biblical teaching on this point, but there is some question about what that is, and this will be discussed later, in the BIBLE section.

Meanwhile, what do scientific facts have to say about human antiquity? Often there are somewhat sensational newspaper or magazine articles about some recent bone or artifact find that "prove" man's age to be so many millions of years. First, we should say that anthropologists are human, and have human weaknesses like the rest of us. Some of them like to have their names in the media. Their reports should be discounted, therefore, until unbiased scholarly confirmation can be had. We should also realize that most media people, and in fact the general public, have long ago accepted evolution as a "fact," and therefore are prone to accept at face value what the new account of any recent scientific discovery is claiming.

Anthropologists have been known to publicly claim a 600,000 year age for a fossil find and later claim a million and three-quarter years age for the same find. A warning is proper here:

> We may attempt to date human remains by the geological conditions of the find, by the associated animal and plant remains, and by implements discovered with them. But this evidence is often difficult to correlate with the glacial time table, and this time table, in turn, is still not firmly established. Hence dates assigned to earlier human finds must be regarded as only tentative in their nature.[7]

The moral to all this is that applying radioactive dating methods of the heavy elements to human remains, or using other similar methods have not proved to be completely precise. When what is dated is lava or other materials found near a fossil find, rather than the fossils themselves, and the relationship between the two has been assumed, we have to recognize that this is not strict science. At any rate, the age of the earth is generally accepted by scientists as four and one-half billion years, and the age of man is, at the most, only two or so million years, as even evolutionists see it. In anyone's view, therefore, man is recent. Also, he is much more recent than animals, which are generally accepted as going back about five hundred million years. Our question, then, is how recent is recent, for man? We begin with a quotation from Wm. F. Albright, who was probably the world's foremost Palestinian archeologist:

> For one thing, it is becoming clear, thanks to the accelerated rate of new finds and the revolution in dating brought by radiocarbon, that only one true species of genus Homo has hitherto been discovered, and that the differences between known types of fossil man have been gravely exaggerated. It is also certain that all known forms of fossil men made tools and probably spoke in different tongues; it is equally clear that the earliest men were inventive and possessed aesthetic tendencies. The antiquity of tool-making is only a fraction of the previous estimates, and may not have exceeded 150,000 - 200,000 years.[8]

We note that Albright, who did not question that there was some sort of evolution, held that man has been here only 150,000 to 200,000 years, while there are some creationists who argue that man has been here longer than that[9]. This shows differences among the creationists as to what the Bible

actually teaches about human antiquity. These differences will
be discussed later.

We would point out that man can be very recent and the
earth and the universe be quite old (if that is what biblical
teaching allows). There are some "scientific" arguments for
human recency that are based on hard archeological facts, and
we now note some of these:

MAN'S TOOLS

Admittedly man, who differs from animals by being a tool-
maker, made his first tools out of stone. It is easy to think of
"the Stone Age" as going back a long time, but most of us will
be shocked to know that the Late Stone Age goes back only to
about 4500 B.C. Stone tools and implements were the only
ones that man had down to this time, as archeologists have
found. The "Bronze Age" for tools, made out of an alloy of
copper and tin, began about 4500 to 4200 B.C. and lasted
until about 1200 B.C. when man began using Iron tools. The
reason for change in all these tools was because of the greater
hardness of the new tools and also their flexibility in usage. The
point is that, however long man has been on the earth, change
in his mental capacity, if any, would have been very slow. *Why
then, with all his intellectual brilliance, did he not learn about
tool-making technology and how to improve it until so very
recently?* This indicates that he actually has not been on the
earth millions of years, or even hundreds of thousands of years.
His existence on earth has surely not been for long. To speak
of it in term of thousands of years fits the known facts better
than the longer periods.

Dr. Albright, the Palestinian archeologist quoted earlier, and
a former teacher of the present writer, said in a personal con-
versation that there has been no discernible change in man's
mental capacity since the days of early fossil men. This being
true, why is it that man's ability to communicate in writing
began as late as 3200 B.C., when Hieroglyphic (picture) writing was first used in the area of Egypt? To have an idea and
communicate with someone by drawing a picture of the idea

(such as drawing a tear to communicate sadness, or drawing a man with distended ribs to indicate famine) is the simplest type of writing possible for intelligent beings. (We say simplest, but in a way such a system is the most complicated, because there must be so many pictures or different characters used, one for each separate idea).

Cuneiform writing, originating in Mesopotamia or Asia Minor and dating about 2200 B.C., was made by making impressions in wet clay with a square stylus and then baking it, and it closely identifies in date with an improvement in writing that introduced syllables, where one character equals a syllable instead of a complete idea. Several syllables can be put together in a word to represent an idea, but the syllables can be used over and over again in other combinations for other words, so that fewer characters are necessary (about 180) for full human communication rather than having to have one character for each idea that you might want to express.

The highest, and the truly simplest, form of writing possible is alphabetic, where with 26 or so characters, in their many possible combinations, one can write anything he wants to. The earliest alphabetic writing that has been found, the Proto-Sinatic characters found in caves in the Sinaitic penisula, dates to about 1790 or so B.C.

What we have in the inception and development of human communication in writing, then, is that between 3200 B.C. and 1800 B.C. (round numbers) man invented writing and then developed it to its highest, yet simplest possible form. This shows man's intellectual brilliance in causing this rapid development, but it also speaks loudly about the fact that he must not have been on earth too much earlier, else he would have developed and perfected writing methods long ago. If he had been here for millions of years, and his mental evolution was gradual, what had he been doing all those earlier years? All this points to

THE RECENCY OF HISTORY

Not only does man's experience in inventing and developing

communication through writing illustrate the probable fact of his recent arrival on the scene, but there are other facts that also indicate this. One is that of his toolmaking and its improvement, as we have already discussed. Another is his habitation experience.

Obviously man would live first in caves, to have protection from the weather, and they were already available. Man's first building of a city to dwell in was probably the city of Jericho in Palestine,[10] the earliest level of which dates about 5000 B.C. according to archeological finds. The small stone tools found with this stratum of occupation were the same as in the last occupation of caves in Palestine, so we know that man's last cave dwelling was done at about this same time. The dating of the early cities is based upon their being built as a mound in strata, one on top of the other, the earliest being the lowest level. The choice of a location for a city was dependent upon a water supply within the walls and the ease of fortification against enemies. When a city was destroyed by fire or war, and a new one was to later be built, the same location was still the best, because of the water and fortifying factors. So the debris was simply leveled off and a new city was built on top of the old one. This continued through the years (the Jericho mound had about twenty strata of occupation in all).

The conclusion called for by these archeological finds concerning man's tools, his writing, and his early habitations, is that human activity on the earth seems to have begun rather suddenly, and within the last few thousand years. Man's history began on several fronts about this time, and we have a "hot trail" of his activities from this time forward. There is a definite increase in the growth of his "civilization" and technical knowledge about this time that is clearly discernible. He learned about fire and the baking of clay vessels and pottery somewhat accidentally, by building a fire at Jericho in a depression in a clay deposit. The fire baked the clay, and when the rain came the depression then held water for a long period. This was the beginning of his manufacture of baked "kitchen pots and pans," and the later development of full-fledged pottery making has since furnished archeologists with the ability to date the several levels of occupation of various city sites.

The big question for our study, however, is that since so many different indications of man's activities in becoming "civilized" began at about the same time, and all very recently, "Where was he?" and, "What was he doing all those previous millions of years that evolution would have him to have been here?" His "hot trail" has surely not covered many years!

11. *The Origin of Mind, Spirit and Values.* Science's domain is the realm of physical things. It has no authority and no special knowledge in the realm of things mental, spiritual or concerning values. Yet if evolution be true, an explanation of where these things came from and how they entered the evolution process is sorely needed. They are realities, and they came from somewhere, somehow. A designer is needed, as even G.G.Simpson has admitted:

> Adaptation is real, and it is achieved by a progressive and directed process. This process is natural, and it is wholly mechanistic in its operation. This natural process achieves the aspect of purpose, without the intervention of a purposer, and it has produced a vast plan, without the concurrent action of a planner. It may be that the initiation of the process and physical laws under which it functions had a Purposer and that this mechanistic way of achieving a plan is the instrument of a Planner — of this still deeper problem the scientist cannot speak.[11]

So Simpson recognizes the logic of the universe needing a designer, even though such a possibility does not appeal to the outlook of evolutionary scientists. The recognition helps us to realize that the existence and action of a Creator God is more logical and is a greater probability than the faith of the person who denies the fact of creation. To believe in God and in the creation is the better faith — it has the needed mechanism that can completely explain the universe as it really is.

Another admission by Simpson is apropos here:

> This is not to say that the whole mystery has been plumbed to its core or that it ever will be. The ultimate mystery is beyond the reach of scientific investigation, and probably of the human mind. There is

neither need nor excuse for postulation of non-material intervention in the origin of life, the rise of man, or any other part of the long history of the material cosmos. Yet the origin of that cosmos and the causal principles of its history remain unexplained and inaccessible to science. Here is hidden the First Cause sought by theology and philosophy. The First Cause is not known and I suspect that it never will be known to living man. We may, if we are so inclined, worship it in our own ways, but we certainly do not comprehend it.[12]

Do we not easily see that evolution is but a faith, rather than a scientific fact, and that creation is the most logical explanation of all the facts that we know?

As to mind, spirit, and values, how could a brain atom think, if it is *only* matter? Is thinking and are ideas real? Are they distinct from the matter of the brain? If a brain cell dies, and its chemicals remain the same for five seconds, has something real departed? What is life, anyway?

What is the unifying principle of a cell of living matter, which adds new atoms of matter to its own structure in the life process and discharges old ones? What is the basis of unity of a human being, whose physical body changes all of its matter atoms for new and fresh matter every five to seven years? What is the nature of the *person*, who remains constant during all of this process? The evolutionist who denies the reality of spirit and spiritual realities is hard put to answer these questions. He also has trouble in explaining and dealing with values — good and bad, right and wrong, true and untrue, beautiful and ugly, faithful and unfaithful, and the millions of other values that make human life to be truly significant and meaningful.

Simpson has confessed that *the search for an absolute ethic, either intuitive or naturalistic, has been a failure.*[13] Likewise T.H.Huxley felt that man's only choices were a "tooth and claw" ethic, or mere survival, or its opposite, that *evolution as a whole is ethically bad.*[14] We see then that evolution has no place in its total worldview for any kind of morality. To the evolutionist, there can be no such thing as good and bad, or right and wrong. For those many people who have been accepting evolution but believe in morality anyway, we are grateful that

134

they are able to choose for values, even though they violate logic in doing so. Values need God.

12. *Punctuated Equilibrium.* Darwin's theory, which got the evolution controversy started, was that evolution was slow and gradual and took a long time. Those who followed his ideas were comfortable in doing so because they argued that "they had all the time" that could be needed. Since he wrote his book in 1859 many hours by many scholars have been spent in studying his theory in all its various aspects.

But the fossil finds have not revealed what evolutionists had hoped. They had wanted to find remains of life forms in continuous sequence of transition from the simple to the complex, all the way from amoeba to man. What they have found, however, is suddenly appearing, fully developed individual organisms in great number, with no indication of any ancestors or transitions from earlier forms. Later, numerous other more complex but still fully developed organisms appear, again with no indication of having come from any previous organisms. Finally man appears, the sequence of appearance of the total of the various life-forms being in moderate concordance with the order of creation as found in Genesis.

The above facts are by now well-known and recognized, so that the most prominent evolutionists of today no longer claim "gradual evolution" but insist that it came in spurts or "bursts," with long periods between when there was no evolution at all. When I wrote in this area about twenty years ago the term for the sudden appearance of new and more complex life forms was called "emergent evolution," which meant that the new forms simply *emerged*, without appearing to have evolved from some other ancestral form. Today's name for this sudden appearance "out of the blue" of new and more complex organisms is "Punctuated Equilibrium," so named by S.J.Gould, paleontologist of Harvard University. It is a repudiation of Darwin's gradualism, but it shows that people who have faith in evolution want to continue to believe in it, even if they have to change arguments why.

N O T E S

1. Huxley, Julian S., "The Evolutionary Vision," in *Evolution After Darwin*, Vol. III, *Issues In Evolution*, Chicago: University of Chicago Press, 1960, p. 249.

2. Moore, John N., "Paleontologic Evidence and Organic Evolution," Special Issue of the Journal of the American Scientific Affiliation on *Origins and Change*, Elgin, Illinois: American Scientific Affiliation, 1978, p. 53.

3. Gilkey, Langdon B., "Darwinism and Christian Thought," *The Christian Century*, January 6, 1960, pp. 8,9.

4. See my book, *Facts and Faith*, Vol.I, Abilene: Abilene Christian University Press, 1966, pp. 188-192.

5. For greater details, see *Ibid*, pp. 131-136; 139-142; 147-151; 189.

6. Huxley, Julian S., *Evolution In Action*, New York: Harper and Brothers, 1953, pp. 41,42.

7. Romer, A.S., *Man and the Vertebrates*, Chicago: University of Chicago Press, 1941, p. 196.

8. Albright, Wm.F., *The Christian Century*, November 19, 1958, p.1329.

9. See my Chart in *Facts and Faith*, Vol. I, p. 137.

10. There have been some indefinite claims of city dwelling in the Mesopotamian valley that date to about 7000 B.C.

11. Simpson, G.G., "The Problem of Plan and Purpose In Nature," *The Scientific Monthly*, LXIV (1947), p.495.

12. Simpson, G.G., *The Meaning of Evolution*, New Haven: Yale University Press, 1949, p. 278.

13. Ibid, p. 310.

14. Ibid, p. 299.

The Bible and Evolution

10

> "The Bible tells us how to go to heaven, not how the heavens go."
> — *GALILEO GALILEI*

THE BIBLE AND ORIGINS

IAN A. FAIR

*P*ossibly due to the experience at the Tower of Babel and other similar clashes with God's purpose, men quickly forgot their divine origin and their roots. Sin clouds one's understanding. The quest for an anchor to the primeval past is a universal concern which has produced numerous attempts to arrive at a sense of beginnings. Without such roots man experiences a sense of incompleteness. These have ranged from the strangely mythological to a variety of evolutionary comcepts. We focus attention upon two attempts to understand origins — evolution and creation.

EVOLUTION

Evolutionary thought has been found as early as 700 B.C., in the early Greek philosophers. Thales, Anaximander, Anaximines, Xenophanes, Heraclitus, Empedocles and others contributed to it, and Aristotle (384-322 B.C.) and Epicurus (342-270 B.C.) gave considerable impetus to the idea, long before Charles Darwin changed modern thinking with his *Origin of the Species* in 1859 A.D. Since Darwin, evolutionary thought has taken on a number of forms and expressions, some of which have gained general acceptance as modern society continues its search for meaning and identity through its quest for its roots.[1] The tragedy is that man, longing for fulfillment, turned his back on the only real solution to his quest, namely, God's personal revelation of himself in history. The words of the Apostle Paul express this most poignantly:

> For what could be known about God is plain to them, because God has shown it to them. Ever since the creation of the world his invisible nature, namely, his eternal power and deity, has been clearly perceived in the things that have been made. So they are without excuse; for although they knew God they did not honor him as God or give thanks to him, but they became futile in their thinking and their senseless minds were darkened. Claiming to be wise, they became fools, and exchanged the glory of the immortal God for images resembling mortal man or birds or animals or reptiles. Therefore God gave them up in the lusts of their hearts to impurity...because they exchanged the truth about God for a lie and worshipped and served the creature rather than the Creator, who is blessed forever.
> —*ROMANS 1:18-25*

For convenience we list and comment briefly on some of the evolutionary theories encountered in the creation-evolution dialogue:

1. *Organic evolution.* This term is used specifically for what we understand to be Darwinian evolution. It holds that the universe came into existence out of nothing by pure chance. Since that "beginning" the universe has slowly evolved through the eons, producing purely by chance development, the complex world of life forms and the universe as we now know them. Such a process requires an extremely old earth (some billions of years) and a process of "uniformitarian development." Julian Huxley, a prominent supporter of this theory, has observed that the process is "A one-way process, irreversible in time...and leading to higher degrees of organization."[2] It is easy to detect G.W.F. Hegel's theory of evolutionary history in this process. One advantage that Hegel had over Darwin and men such as Huxley is that Hegel did hold to an "Absolute

Infinite Spirit" (however he may have conceived it) or power of some sort guiding the process and giving it its upward mobility and continual "progress." J.D.Thomas has succinctly defined evolution as "The view that all life came from very simple life forms, by natural process only."[3]

The theory of evolution, as we have already noted, is not modern, since it dates back to as early as 700 B.C. It was Darwin's impact, however, claiming "natural selection and survival of the fittest," and aided by Hegel's philosophy, that caused the theory to come to public attention. Even though evolution has received much attention through the years, it still lacks an efficient driving mechanism. Without such a definite mechanism, however, evolution must remain an unproven theory. Evolution remains an attempt to artificially piece together scientific facts and to postulate or extrapolate from them a theory of origins. The conclusions of the theory reach beyond science into speculative philosophy, and this is why it can never be truly considered scientific fact, in spite of large numbers of people now believing it to be so.

2. *Theistic Evolution.* It is clear that the basic theory of organic evolution is in direct conflict with Genesis and Biblical creation, since it relies on pure chance and has no mechanism. It denies the existence and the necessity of a divine being. Because this is so, some wishing to maintain a semblance of faith in Genesis and in God have attempted to blend a theory of evolution with creation — thus Theistic evolution. They desire to be Biblical, but fail because they attempt to force their exegesis through the "projection lens" of contemporary evolutionary theory, surrendering any hope of truly being Biblical. The effort of Theistic evolution to compromise faith in God with organic evolution possibly has a heritage reaching back to Augustine (354-430 A.D.). Some evidence indicates that Thomas Aquinas (1225-1274 A.D.) was aware of such views.[4] The recent popularity of the theistic view, however, has no doubt come from the fact that many "believers" have made, that "organic evolution had been proved as a fact," as

evolutionists claim. In holding to theistic evolution, these "believers" consequently desire to have "both faith and fact."

Theistic evolutionists believe that God was responsible for the initial creation of matter, but that he then permitted the matter to evolve through the normal evolutionary process. The real difference between this and organic evolution is that God has been introduced in the place of chance, and that He is the guiding spirit behind the process, all the while maintaining scientific credibility. As to man's unique qualities, when the animal side of man developed sufficiently, God then "breathed into him the breath of life" and he became a spiritual human being.[5]

A major problem with this theory is that it is simply not Biblical! No stretch of the imagination can square theistic evolution with Genesis 1 and 2, for it is simply impossible to reconcile this theory with any true exegetical method or concept of Biblical theology.[6]

3. *Progressive Creation*. Believers in Biblical creation are uncomfortable with theistic evolutionary theory because its inclination is more in the direction of evolution than creation. There is another view, called "progressive creation," which wants to lean more in the direction of creation, yet maintain a "progressive" view of development, or evolution. Those who hold to progressive creation suggest that while life was developing along the vast line of evolutionary progress, God, at certain points, by fiat action, created certain life forms, permitting them then to develop further by the normal evolutionary process. They believe that this process accounts for much of the fossil and geological evidence claimed by organic evolutionists, and also for *the sudden appearance* of new forms of life. In other words, the fossil forms as we actually find them are explained by the *horizontal* development of evolution, and the sudden appearances of new forms are explained by the *vertical* activity of God. The popularity of the progressive creation idea is probably due to the influence of Bernard Ramm, who observed:

> Progressive creation tries to avoid the arbitrariness of fiat creationism
> and preserve its doctrine of the transcendence of God in creation; and
> it has tried to avoid the uniformitarianism of theistic evolution, and
> preserve its sense of progressive development.[7]

The Biblical theologian's problem with progressive creation
is much the same as with theistic evolution — *it is simply not
Biblical.* It attempts to impose an evolutionary grid over creation that is completely alien to the Biblical text. One cannot
deny that change has occurred in the development of certain
life forms, but that these are best explained by "the evolutionary process" should be closely questioned. To argue from
Genesis 1 and 2 that God, at certain points in the evolutionary
process, by fiat creation, brought new life forms into being,
leaving them to "evolve," is a highly speculative stretch of
exegetical imagination, hardly befitting Biblical theology.

CREATION

In contrast with the evolutionary model of origins, Biblical
theists have long held that Biblical creation as described in
Genesis 1 and 2 is the most efficient, simple, and coherent
model available to human thought. Creation naturally is a
matter of faith, but faith is not the taking of a radical risk *in the
absence of any evidence!* Faith is not just a blind leap in the
dark! The Judaeo-Christian faith has always been one built on
the historical evidence of God's activity in history. From the
early days of its faith, Israel described God in terms of what he
had done for her in history!

The central problem faced by the Judaeo-Christian faith
regarding origins is that of the proper interpretation of Genesis
1 and 2. Those who believe in creation are not all agreed on
every detail, leading to various "schools of thought" among
them. A chief problem is that some attempt to do their exegesis through the lens of contemporary scientific theories. This
creates problems when scientific theories advance into new
areas and to new conclusions. Lacking any consistent scientific

lens, such creation theories reflect the nature of a kaleidoscope without any consistent form.

We are limited by space but we need to consider a few of the interpretations of Genesis 1 and 2:

1. *Concordism.* This approach attempts to find agreements between Biblical faith and science, emphasizing their similarities. Such a view wants to treat the Bible as a sort of inspired scientific textbook, finding accurate scientific references where the original author was surely unaware of any such implications. What concordism fails to consider is the fact that the Bible was given in a Pre-Copernican scientific world-view to a people not really impressed by science. For God to intentionally couch his word in scientific terms would immediately create problems in a world whose scientific understanding was limited and changing. That God's word was couched in terms that draw on a specific world-view is natural, since it was given to real people living in a real world, facing real worldly problems and with the real world-view of that day. Any "scientific" references would, therefore, be purely incidental and not a part of the basic warp and woof of the message.

The strength of concordism is that it seeks for a coherence between science and scripture, with an underlying commitment to scripture. A problem with it, however, is that it tends to read contemporary scientific views into scripture, and thus becomes untenable because scientific knowledge changes. This view does not allow scripture its own perspective, and the right to stand in its own historical context.

2. *Anti-Scientism.* This view is an over-reaction against science to the extent that its adherents erect their own "scientific system," which tends to the same extreme of speculation as that of some of the evolutionary scientists they oppose. The anti-scientists are often extreme literalists who do not have access to adequate facts, and who manifest little true exegetical skill. Their conclusions are, therefore, somewhat narrow and brittle and fail to consider the nuances of the literary genre.

We should, therefore, beware of those who interpret scripture through a scientific grid (concordism), or in opposition to a scientific grid (anti-scientism). Both are alien to the genius of scripture, and neither gives adequate attention to the richness of the full range of the literary genre in scripture.

3. *Fideism.* This term derives from the Latin *fides,* meaning faith, and it places much emphasis on "trust." This emphasis leads its devotees to ignore science and reason, insisting that faith is unrelated to historical or scientific evidences. Fideism attempts to separate faith from the realm of history or science, making faith the product of the will, or the activity of the Holy Spirit.

Both Biblical faith and Fideism recognize that the Bible is not a book of science but one of religious faith and practice. But they differ in that Fideism does not allow history, nature and science to have any part in the development of faith, whereas Biblical theology does. In fact Biblical faith is not at all opposed to any contribution that history or science might lend in support of the development of faith. Biblical theology, however, recognizes that it is Scripture and not science or reason that is the fundamental foundation for faith. For the Biblical theologian to turn away from history is to close his eyes to the true nature of Scripture.[8] Likewise, for the Fideist to eschew all apologetic argument in support of faith is therefore un-Biblical.

4. *Reconstruction Theory.* This theory is sometimes called the "gap theory," and comes in a variety of forms. Basically these theories attempt to fit the extreme ages of the earth suggested by some scientists into the meaning of Genesis 1:1-3, by suggesting a gap between the original creation of Genesis 1:1,2 and the creative days of 1:3ff. According to this view, millions of years ago in the primordial past, God created the universe but it was without form, in some sort of a gaseous mass. Genesis 1:3ff describes the "reconstruction" or reorganization of this nebulous universe into the solid universe as we now know

it. Reconstruction theories make much of the seeming break between Genesis 1:2 and 1:3.

The problem we encounter with this method is much the same as that in Concordism, namely, that it superimposes scientific interests on Biblical interpretation as though the text must manifest scientific concerns. Reconstruction theories simply do not give adequate attention to the Biblical text itself, and they manifest more concern for the evolution-science dialogue than they do for the syntax of the Genesis text itself. Willis comments on the difficulty of translating these verses and the supposed break between them in saying:

> Accordingly, the best biblical linguists translate this term (bere'shith IAF) "In the beginning of God's creating [or when God began to create] the heavens and the earth, the earth was without form and void." (d) On the other hand, if it is connected with verse 3, verse 2 must be interpreted as a parenthesis, and one would read: "In the beginning of God's creating the heavens and the earth (the earth being without form and void, etc.), God said, Let there be light, etc."" This last interpretation seems to be best in keeping with the syntax of the Massoretic text (MT).[9]

It is only when one has to find a long period of time in the creation process to account for the great antiquity of the earth and problems with uniformitarianism that one has to force one's exegesis of Genesis 1:1-3 to accomodate this. This seems to be farthest from Moses' mind in Genesis 1:1-3. Willis has shown that such reconstruction theories are not in keeping with the syntax of the passage.

5. *Day-Age Theory.* This theory suggests a solution for many in the "impasse" found in the creation-evolution dialogue. It suggests that the creative days in Genesis 1:3ff are not necessarily 24-hour days, but could be interpreted to mean an undetermined age or time period. By adopting such an interpretation, one can easily (it is claimed) fit the long periods of the scientific ages, demanded by uniformitarianism, into the Biblical account of creation. While it is possible to consider the term "day" in the Hebrew language to mean "time" or "age," this does seem to strain the simplest interpretation of Genesis 1:3ff. We will

146

notice below that the Biblical theologian should have no difficulty with the "24-hour day" interpretation *if the text is permitted to speak in its own literary context and within its own purpose* in the unity and diversity of Biblical theology, and not in the context of the creation-evolution debate which was alien to Moses and Israel and their peculiar needs at the time of this writing.

There are a number of similar "day" theories, all intending to deal with the problem of harmonizing the Genesis account of creation with modern scientific interests. All manifest the same problems encountered in the day-age theory; all seek to interpret the Biblical text through a superimposed scientific grid. In doing so they show little regard for sound exegesis and Biblical theology.

THE THEOLOGY OF GENESIS

We have examined several views of origins, commenting on their strengths and weaknesses from the perspective of a Biblical theologian. Most of the problems encountered by each, consist in that they have attempted to be Biblical, while overlaying the text with a contemporary scientific grid. When the Biblical text is projected through a scientific lens it loses its Biblical perspective.

To properly interpret Genesis one should let it stand in its own unique context and we should overlay only the religious, sociological and historical context of the text itself. We recognize that presuppositionless exegesis is not possible. Our chief concern, therefore, should be the validity of our own presuppositions. It is the conviction of this writer that a "scientific" concern or presupposition is not the proper context out of which to do Biblical exegesis. The only presupposition one should bring to exegesis is the view that Scripture is the inspired word of God, and that as Scripture it should be permitted to stand in its own literary, historical, and religious context.

A. *Diversity of the Theological Message in Genesis.*

The diversity of concern and emphasis of the individual books of the Bible is held in dynamic tension by the overarching unity of the Biblical message. This unity of Biblical message concerns the revelation of God's person and nature and of his plan of reconciliation of sinful man. This tension of individual diversity and overall unity is a fundamental concern for the Biblical interpreter. Any attempt at interpretation that is not sensitive to this tension will lead to an abuse of the text. Every text must be considered in the light of its immediate context (the diversity of message in the individual book) and the larger context (the unity of the Biblical passage). When the creation text is divorced from the immediate historical and theological context of Genesis, or when Genesis is forced into a context of scientific concern alien to the overall unity of Biblical message regarding God's personal revelation and reconciliation, the creation text is subjected to extreme abuse.

1. *The Unique Historical Context and Theme of Genesis.*
The clearest meaning of Genesis can be found when it stands in the framework of the revelation of God, man's tendency to sin, and God's scheme of redemption. In this context we learn of Israel's faith issues, and of her search for identity — not of some historical or scientific concern. Israel's religious development and faith are the primary concerns.

2. *The Biblical interpreter should seek to know what the inspired Moses had in mind as he wrote the Pentateuch* (the first five books of the law). What compelling influence drove him to write of the divine origin of man and his universe? What motivation did he have to cause him to discuss the fall of man and God's covenants with Abraham and his descendants?
    Israel's historical context at the time of Moses' writing reveals an amazing set of circumstances. Under his leadership they had just experienced the Exodus — deliverance from 400 years of bondage in Egypt. They now stood at the threshold of a new existence, barely conscious of being God's chosen

people. They had almost forgotten God's covenant with Abraham and had adopted many pagan customs and religious habits. Moses' struggle with them over the golden calf incident indicates the depth of this Egyptian enculturation. Although remnants of the faith of Abraham, Isaac and Jacob were still there, Israel in Egypt had become a pagan people, having adopted much of the Egyptian polytheistic pantheon. At Mount Sinai God renewed his covenant with his people and began the painful process of reeducating them and refocusing their faith. Any interpretation of Genesis or other books of Moses must take this historical context into account in order to understand the genius of the book.

As Israel and Moses struggled with their newly found freedom, they faced the need to restructure their sense of national and personal identity, and their social and religious obligations. Genesis emphasized the divine origin of the universe, and man's roots in the creative activity of God, rather than in the nature of pagan mythology. It reveals the nature of God's person, man's need of redemption from his sins, and God's scheme for that redemption. To divorce Genesis from this context and this purpose, or even to relegate them to a secondary interest, would be to surrender one's claim to Biblical interpretation.

2. Relating this Unique Emphasis to the Unity of the Biblical Message.

The central message of the Bible is the revelation of God and his plan of redemption, while the unique theological emphasis in Genesis develops the theme of Israel's "beginnings" or "generations." The interpreter should hold these emphases in dynamic tension and demonstrate how the unique theme of Genesis relates to the central Biblical message, namely, the revelation of God and his reconciliation of sinful man. Setting Genesis and the Pentateuch in the context of Israel's struggles with its personal identity and faith connects Israel's faith back to its origins with the one God, the powerful Creator of the universe; to its beginnings and the centrality of God's plan of reconciliation; to God's covenants with Abraham, Isaac and Jacob. By setting Israel's roots into God's creative activity, his scheme of redemption, and deliverance from Egypt, Moses integrates Israel's existence and faith into the overall theme of God's revelation and redemptive activity. A sound exegetical method will keep this dynamic relationship of diversity and unity of theological message in mind when considering the context out of which to move in the exegetical procedure.

B. *The Word of God in Genesis.*

The message of God that reaches out from Genesis is that Israel is different from the nations round about. She should know that her roots go back to the powerful Creator and only God of the universe; that her deliverance from Egypt is nothing less than an expression of his loving concern for her, already manifest in God's covenant with Abraham and his active role in Israel's history through the patriarchs. Genesis serves to remind Israel of her uniqueness as the chosen people of God, and to give the young nation a sense of personal identity, without which no one can survive in this hostile world. Genesis shows that God's redemptive power is directly related to his creative power. He is the same God who created the heavens and the earth, and that now delivers Israel and calls her to be his chosen people.

INTERPRETING GENESIS 1 AND 2

Interpreting scripture is as hazardous today as it has ever been. Most disagreements between Christians are not in using different scriptures, but in the models of interpretation which they bring to the text. This is especially true in regard to Genesis 1 and 2. Well meaning believers sometimes tend to make their personal convictions and fine points of interpretation the basis of acceptance by God. This is an unfortunate attitude, but it dramatizes the necessity of using a sound exegetical method. Aristotle is reported to have said, "It is not the facts which

divide men but the interpretation of the facts."[10] The facts of
Genesis 1 and 2 seem to be quite clear — the almighty God
created the heavens and the earth and all that are in them. This
clarity, however, does not always come through clearly in our
concern for interpreting Genesis 1 and 2. Other issues, such as
evolution or theistic evolution, are introduced and cloud this
clarity. Hummell aptly points out the importance of the intention of the text when seeking to interpret and understand.

> Much of the controversy arises from a misunderstanding of what the
> Genesis account of creation intends to teach. What message was it
> meant to convey to ancient Israel in their struggle against the pagan
> mythologies of the surrounding countries? How does that meaning
> apply in a post-Christian culture whose gods and values infiltrate even
> the church?[11]

We need to keep reminded that there is an ever present tendency to lay grids over the text other than the simple intention
that Genesis plays in the faith of Israel and the revelation of
God's person and plan of reconciliation. We must not introduce contemporary scientific concerns that cloud the clarity of
this intention. We should attempt only to see the Genesis text
through the eyes of an Israelite living in Moses' day, and we
should strive only to determine what Moses *intended* them to
understand.

A. *The Literary Genre of Genesis 1 and 2.*

Since we have already determined the historical and religious
context of Genesis, we should consider the literary genre (or
literary type) of the writing. What kind of literature is this that
we are concerned with? Is it prose or poetry; historical narrative
or parable; is it literal or figurative?

Liberal theologians for the past two centuries have considered the Pentateuch to be a composite work, the result of
different theological interests in developing stages. Under the
rubric of *the documentary hypothesis* these theologians feel that
they can identify the hand of different authors in these works.

Conservative scholars, on the other hand, consider Moses to have been the writer.[12]

The style of Genesis is neither careless nor patchwork, but carefully designed and powerful in its simplicity. Critical study of the text of the first two chapters reveals a deliberate, tightly knit structure. Clearly, the text is not simply poetry, but it does manifest a repetition and a movement that lifts it above normal narrative style to a unique structure. Its genius as a unique literary genre, and an awareness of this genius, helps one understand the author's interest and intention.

Furthermore, our text sensitively handles the complex problem of describing God's being and his divine activity, which are difficult for human language and understanding. Man ordinarily resorts to anthropomorphisms in such cases — speaking of God in human terms; of his voice, his face, his working or his resting. This approach does not infer that the events of his activity did not occur, but simply that man has to resort to human analogy, or figurative language, in order to comprehend God's nature and ways.[13]

Again, the Hebrew language differs from modern western languages which tend toward an analytical and mathematical precision. Hebrew and other eastern languages use a synthetic approach, using parallelism, synonym, and rhythm for dramatic description. The tight structure of Genesis 1 and 2, with its unique parallelism, drawing on the strengths of Hebrew style, emphasizes in simple clarity the dramatic power of the message.[14]

Although Genesis 1 and 2 describes God's creative activity in anthropomorphic analogy, it still is classifiable as a "historical" narrative, that is, a narrative describing real activity. It is not a poem or story in the form of legend or myth, but is a "historical" narrative of God's creative activity in anthropomorphic, analogous language in carefully structured literary form.[15]

If Genesis uses anthropomorphic analogy is it correct to speak of a literal interpretation of its first two chapters? The answer is a resounding, Yes! Pure narration is not the only literary form that can be literal! To describe God's creative activity demands analogy, for we do find such parallels to divine activity in our ordinary human experiences. But resorting to analogy does not detract from the fact that the activity actually happened! All that this says is that the divine activity is described in anthropomorphic analogy. Hummel observes: "A stringent literalism disregards the analogical medium of revelation about creation, raising meaningless questions about God's working schedule.[16]

Moses' literary artistry is seen in his stylistic structuring of Genesis 1:1-31 around eight (8) "creative word" expressions and six (6) "creative days." This is set out in two parallel sections around the creative words, "And God said, 'Let the...." Notice how the four (4) "creative word" expressions and three (3) "creative days" balance each other in the two sections.

CREATIVE WORDS	DAY	ELEMENT:
1 "And God said, Let..." (vs.3)	1	LIGHT
2 "And God said, Let..." (vs.6)	2	FIRMAMENT
3 "And God said, Let..." (vs.9)	3	SEAS
4 "And God said, Let..."		LAND AND VEGETATION
5 "And God said, Let..." (vs.14)	4	LUMINARIES
6 "And God said, Let..." (vs.20)	5	BIRDS
7 "And God said, Let..."	6	FISHES
8 "And God said, Let..."		ANIMAL & MAN

(— Adapted from Hummel, *The Galileo Connection*, p.205)

The closely structured literary design of this text, with the eight statements "And God said, Let...." in association with the enormous creative activity of the six days, draws attention to the dynamic power of God's creative word. Willis also comments on this tight literary structure, noticing that the column on the left, namely the first three days, indicates the "habitation" of the creatures in the column on the right.

Careful attention to the literary structure described above emphasizes the literary artistry and interest of Moses.

Awareness of this carefully designed structure indicates that literary concern seems to dominate any purely historical or scientific interest. The literary design dramatizes, and thus plays an important role in the creation narrative. To fail to take account of this characteristic of the text results in a limited understanding of Moses' powerful message. Emphasis on the literary interest of the text need not imply a denial of the historical reality of creation, it merely draws attention to the fact that the prime interest is literary dramatization rather than mere historical concern.

B. *The Six Days of Creation.*

Much has been written regarding the six days of creation. Do they simply refer to a literal six 24-hour days? Is this a reference to a figurative period of many centuries, or is it simply poetical language? Elsewhere this book will deal with these topics, but the simple reading of the text seems to indicate a 24-hour, solar day. To this writer it seems most likely that it would have been the obvious interpretation of Moses' readers to render the term *day* in this fashion. Creation is described in the analogy of six day's work and one day of rest. This would be the natural interpretation to the original reader. This, in the context of the literary structure and emphasis of the text, would be a clear statement to Israel that the earth did not come into being by chance, or by the ingenuity of some pagan gods. The origin of the earth and the purposeful creation of man was by none other than the God who had brought them by his own hand out of the land of Egypt. Later references in the Pentateuch to six days' work followed by a seventh day of rest would remind Israel of their divine origin, and that their existence was due to none other than the almighty Creator, Yahweh. The six days' work and sabbath rest would be a memorial reminder of their divine origin. They were his created and his chosen people.

The simple, yet powerful nature of the creation account, described in eight creative bursts of power over six days would raise no questions of a scientific nature in the minds of the original readers. The simple statement of their origin connected them directly with the creative power of the one true God, Yahweh. For an interpreter of today to make something out of this account that speaks to a contemporary scientific theory is to do an injustice to the text.

C. *The Supposedly "Two" Creation Accounts.*

The reading of Genesis 1 and 2 may leave an impression that there are two separate accounts of creation. Liberal scholars tend to postulate that the author(s) (?) of Genesis conflated two different accounts in the creation narrative. Resorting to a view holding to two disparate accounts need not be necessary. Willis has observed contrary to such views that the first account (Genesis 1:1 - 2:3) is "a panoramic description of creation," in which the *overall* emphasis is given to God's creative activity. Genesis 2:4 - 25 is "a more *detailed* [emphasis mine IAF] description of the creation of man" in which attention is drawn to the fact that God carefully created man and provided for him all that he needed for life, including a partner suitable for his unique needs.

D. *The Meaning and Significance of Genesis 1 and 2.*

Set in the context of Israel's deliverance from Egypt and consequent search for identity in a world of idolatry, Genesis was a tremendous factor in building Israel's faith in the one true God of the universe. It served in developing a monotheistic faith in the presence of Israel's polytheistic neighbors. Each creative act was a direct challenge to, and a negation of, the nature gods of Israel's neighbors. Each creative act reminded Israel of the power, the love, and the concern of the God who delivered her. It was not necessary for Israel to know precisely *how* he had achieved his creative activity! What Israel needed to know more than anything else was the Creator himself, his power, his love, and his deliverance.

> Oh sing to the Lord a new song; sing to the Lord all the earth!
> Sing to the Lord, bless his name;
> tell of his salvation from day to day.
> Declare his glory among the nations,

his marvelous works among all the peoples!
For great is the Lord,
and greatly to be praised;
he is to be feared above all gods.
For all the gods of the peoples are idols;
but the Lord made the heavens.

PSALM 96: 1-5

E. *Conclusion.*

The simplicity, power, and majesty of the Genesis statement are obvious — our earthly and human origins are the result of the direct and personal action of Jehovah, the Almighty God; the God who spoke, and it was so. Our personal identity and dignity are established; we are of God, he who by his infinite sovereign power and word is the Creator and Sustainer of life.

O the depth of the riches and wisdom and knowledge of God!
How unsearchable are his judgments and how inscrutable are his ways!
For who has known the mind of the Lord, or who has been his counselor?
Or who has given a gift to him that he might be repaid?
For from him and through him are all things.
To him be the glory for ever. Amen.

ROMANS 11:33-36

Hummel has summarized and emphasized the significance of the creation account for our overall understanding of God's redemption:

The doctrine of creation is foundational for God's providential care for his creation, for his redemption of humanity and for his re-creation of a new heaven and earth. Its teaching of God's transcendent sovereignty and power is embodied in a hymn in the last book of the Bible:

"You are worthy, our Lord and our God,
to receive glory and honor and power,
for you created all things,
And by your will they were created
and have their being."

REVELATION 4:11

We conclude with the simple statement that God's creative power, so simply yet powerfully described in Genesis 1 and 2, is absolutely and inextricable connected to the redemption of man. His sovereign power to save stands upon his sovereign power to create. To direct interpretation up a side street chasing scientific concerns is to detour interpretation into a dead end, there to miss the beauty and the power of the Genesis account.

N O T E S

---

1. For a more detailed and balanced discussion of the history and problems of evolution, cf. J.D.Thomas, *Facts and Faith, Vol.I*, pp. 108-187; Paul A. Zimmerman, ed., Darwin, Evolution, and Creation; John W. Klotz, Studies in Creation; Arlie J. Hoover, Fallacies of Evolution.

2. Julian S. Huxley, "At Random," Evolution After Darwin, Vol.III, *Issues In Evolution*, Chicago: Univ. of Chicago Press, 1960, p.42.

3. J.D.Thomas, *op.cit.* p.291.

4, Thomas Aquinas, *Summa Theologica*, Vol. I, New York: Random House, 1945, pp. 45-46, 65-74.

5. See J.D.Thomas, *op.cit.*, p.177, for comments on this.

6. Biblical exegesis and theology move out of a critical study of the text *in its own context*. The historical, sociological, and theological context of Israel in no manner suggests contemporary scientific concerns, but solely Israel's need to understand itself as a nation delivered by the one true God who created the earth and man himself. Israel is to worship and serve the one true God of creation, not the polytheistic gods of Egypt and her new Canaanite neighbors. Genesis sets Israel directly into the line of God's saving history stretching from the primeval creation, through Abraham to Moses and the Exodus. The concern is religious and relates to faith matters, not contemporary scientific concerns. Any concept of theistic evolution, or attempt to reconcile creation with scientific concerns is arbitrary and not in keeping with true Biblical exegesis and theology.

7. Ramm, Bernard, *The Christian View of Science and Scripture*, Grand Rapids: Wm.B.Eerdmans, 1954, pp.76-78.

8. Cf. Romans 1:19,20, where Paul argues that the Gentiles are without excuse because they not only rejected the personal revelation of God himself, but also the corroborating revelation of nature.

9. John Willis, *Genesis.* p. 79.

10. Cited in Hummel, *The Galileo Connection*, p.23.

11. Ibid, p.199.

12. Cf. John Willis, *op.cit.* for a discussion of this point. Willis shows the failure of the documentary hypothesis to adequately handle the contents,

style, and authorship of the Pentateuch. The above comment does not mean that one cannot detect *in extant manuscripts* the hand of later scribes. The manuscripts are of considerable antiquity and we are not the first to work with them. It is the task of textual critics to unravel the complexities of these ancient documents. We can be satisfied, however, that we have in Genesis essentially what Moses wrote under the revealing and inspiring power of the Holy Spirit.

13. Although the western scientific mind is not always comfortable with figurative language, one should not be afraid of such, inferring that figurative language is inferior, or less truthful. When speaking of God, or describing God's activity, one is forced to resort to figurative anthropomorphic analogy. Such language describes God's activity in the most dramatic manner.

14. For detailed discussion of the tight, yet powerful structure of the creation account in Genesis, Cf. Hummel, op. cit. pp. 203-205, where he speaks of the simplicity and economy of language in the text; and cf. also Willis, *op. cit.*, p. 78f.

15. Genesis manifests none of the characteristics of creation mythology current in Moses' day, and should not, therefore, be described as myth. In religious language, myth carries a connotation far removed from the nature or style of Genesis. We have chosen to speak of "historical" narrative in the technical use of the term historical. Relating to matters of primeval history before the advent of time or man one should not technically speak simply of history. We use the term "history," however, in that it is describing events that actually took place in God's creative activity.

16. Hummel, *op. cit.*, p. 215.

BIBLIOGRAPHY

Blocher, Henri, *In The Beginning*. Downer's Grove: InterVarsity Press, 1984.

Hoover, Arlie J., *Fallacies of Evolution*. Grand Rapids: Baker Book House, 1977.

Hummel, Charles E., *The Galileo Connection*. Downer's Grove: InterVarsity Press, 1986.

Klotz, John W., *Studies in Creation*. St.Louis: Concordia Publishing House, 1985.

Morris, Henry M. *The Troubled Waters of Evolution*. San Diego: Creation-Life Publishers, 1974.

Newman, Robert, and Eckelmann, Herman J. Jr., *Genesis One and the Origin of the Earth*. Downer's Grove: InterVarsity Press, 1977.

Shute, Evan, *Flaws in the Theory of Evolution.* Grand Rapids: Baker Book House, 1961.

Thomas, J.D., *Facts and Faith, Vol.I,* Abilene: ACU Press, 1966.

Willis, John T., *Genesis.* Abilene: ACU Press, 1979.

Young, Edward J., *Studies in Genesis One.* Philadelphia: Presbyterian and Reformed Publishing Co., 1964.

Zimmerman, Paul A., *Darwin, Evolution and Creation.* St.Louis: Concordia Publishing House, 1959.

11

THE WEEK OF CREATION

NEIL R. LIGHTFOOT

*U*ntil rather recent times, most people in Europe and America found their explanation of the origin of things in the first words of the Bible: "In the beginning God created heaven and earth." But these words are not as familiar as they once were, and now many people are turning to general encyclopedia articles for answers to questions on life. One may go, for example, to the recent edition of *Encyclopedia Britannica* and read the article entitled, "Myths and Doctrines of Creation," with all that the title of the article implies. Or, again, if one chooses to read in the same encyclopedia the article on "Evolution," he is met with an immediate broadside of misinformation so dogmatically stated that surely hardly anyone would dare to contravene it.

For illustrative purposes, it might be well to summarize and quote from the opening lines of this article on evolution:

> Man's interest in his own origin is as old as himself. "It is reflected in literary form . . . in legends of creation popular among the peoples of antiquity — Sumerians, Egyptians, Greeks, and Hebrews, whose sacred book, the Old Testament, contains two descriptions of the creation and traces of a third." Primitive people naturally ascribed the

creation of things to their deities. "This is the reason that problems
surrounding the origin of the earth . . . were wrapped in unquestioned
and unquestionable dogmas." Only comparatively recently have such
dogmas come under question. "The Copernican system dethroned the
geocentric view of the universe. Evolution . . . has led to an even more
profound revolution . . . . Evolution is the kernel of biology. It is
significant that, before Charles Darwin established evolution as an
inescapable fact and showed how it was brought about . . . ."

The above shows how one-sided the article is in its viewpoint,
and also how three events in the last half of the nineteenth
century emerged to challenge the Biblical account of creation.
One challenge came in the 1870s and afterward from the
comparative religionists, who pointed to similarities in Genesis
with ancient myths of creation, leaving the impression that the
Hebrew version of creation was but another folktale of the
Near East. Another challenge came in 1878, with the publica-
tion of J. Wellhausen's *Prolegomena to the History of Ancient
Israel.* In this Wellhausen argues that there are two different
accounts of creation in Genesis 1 and 2, and that the two
accounts are contradictory to each other. Another challenge,
earlier and of wider extent, came in 1859 with Charles
Darwin's *Origin of the Species.* Darwin's evolutionary hypothesis, if true, made the Genesis creation account false, or, at least,
not literally true. All three of these challenges to Genesis are
blurred together in the *Britannica* article, along with the
enormous statement of error that Darwin had demonstrated
how evolution had occurred.

Contrary to the article on evolution, it is not a foregone con-
clusion that Genesis is of little value on the origin of things.
No such *a priori* judgment should be pronounced on Genesis.
Indeed, it may be possible by a careful examination of the
Biblical text to clear up considerable misapprehension about
what Genesis does and does not say. A detailed exegesis of the
creation acccount(s) in Genesis 1 and 2 is not possible here.
Instead, I propose to sketch some of the important features of
"The Week of Creation" as given in chapter 1, especially since
this raises many of the key problems on origins; and then I

wish to address some of these problems. My approach, though selective in scope, will be strictly exegetical: the text, if it illuminates any obscure matter, must be allowed to speak for itself and to interpret itself.

OPENING VERSES OF CHAPTER ONE

"In the beginning God . . . " is the first and basic affirmation of the Biblical text. No attempt is made to prove God's existence or to define Him in any way. The text accepts that He is and that He does — He created "heaven and earth." "Heaven and earth" is a characteristic Hebrew expression that stands for the cosmos, the entire universe.

It is possible to take Genesis 1:1 either as a dependent clause or as an independent clause. The distinction in meaning may be seen, for example, by comparing the Revised Standard Version (also the KJV and the ASV) with the New English Bible:

In the beginning God created the heavens and the earth. The earth was without form and void, and darkness was upon the face of the deep....And God said, "Let there be light... (RSV)

In the beginning of creation, when God made heaven and earth, the earth was wihtout form and void, with darkness over the face of the abyss....God said, "let there be light"...(NEB; cf. Moffatt's translation).

Even other renderings of these opening verses are possible. It is not necessary to discuss the various meanings of the original Hebrew in order to see the differences in the translations. As an independent clause, the statement is simply that God created all things. As a dependent clause, when God created everything, the earth was formless and empty. Of course, the difference between the two is considerable; but viewed in terms of other Biblical statements, there can be no doubt that Scripture plainly teaches that God is Creator in the real and ultimate sense. Later, Genesis speaks of "God Most High," and as "maker of heaven and earth (14:19,22). Other declarations of Scripture to the same effect are many and impressive:

> For in six days the Lord made heaven and earth, the sea, and all that is in them. *Exodus 20:11.*

> Thou art the Lord, thou alone; that hast made heaven, the heaven of heavens, with all their host, the earth and all that is on it, the seas and all that is in them; and thou preservest all of them . . . . *Nehemiah 9:6.*

> Where were you when I laid the foundation of the earth? Job 38:4. When I look at thy heavens, the works of thy fingers, the moon and the stars which thou hast established . . . . *Psalm 8:3.*

> By the word of the Lord the heavens were made, and all their host by the breath of his mouth . . . . For he spoke, and it came to be; he commanded, and it stood forth.

> Before the mountains were brought forth, or ever thou hadst formed the earth and the world, from everlasting to everlasting thou art God. *Psalm 90:2.*

> The Lord by wisdom founded the earth; by understanding he established the heavens. *Proverbs 3:19.*

> Thus says God the Lord, who created the heavens and stretched them out, who spread forth the earth and what comes from it, who gives breath to the people upon it and spirit to those who walk in it. . . . . *Isaiah 42:5.*

> For lo, he who forms the mountains, and creates the wind, and declares to man what is his thought; who makes the morning darkness, and treads on the heights of the earth — the Lord, the God of hosts, is his name. *Amos 4:13.*

> Have we not all one father? Has not one God created us? *Malachi 2:10.*

> In the beginning was the word . . . . all things were made through him, and without him was not anything made that was made. *John 1:1-3.*

> The God who made the world and everything in it, being Lord of heaven and earth . . . gives to all men life and breath and everything. *Acts 17:24,25.*

> Yet for us there is one God, the Father, from whom are all things and for whom we exist, and one Lord, Jesus Christ, through whom are all things and through whom we exist. *1 Corinthians 8:6.*

> By faith we understand that the world was created by the word of God, so that what is seen was made out of things which do not appear. *Hebrews 11:3.*

In addition, there are numerous other sections of Biblical teaching on creation: Gen. 1:1-2:9; 2:18-25; 1 Sam. 2:8; Job 12:10; 26:7; 37:18; 38:7-11; Psalm 19:1-4; 65:6; 74:16,17; 89:11,12; 95:4,5; 104; 136:5-9; 148:5; Prov. 8:25-31; Eccl.3:11; Isa. 40:12; 26-28; 44:24; 45:7-12; 48:13; 51:13; 66:2; Jer. 5:22; 10:12; 27:5; 31:35; 32:176; 51:15,16; Amos 5:8; 9:6; Jonah 1:9; Zech. 12:1; John 1:10; Acts 14:15; 17:24-26; 28; Rom. 4:17; 11:33-36; 2 Cor. 4:6; Col. 1:16,17; Heb. 1:2; 10,11; 2:10; 3:4; Rev. 4:11; 10:6. God as Creator is a fundamental fact and presupposition of Scripture, and Genesis 1:1 must be understood in this light.

Genesis 1:2 records three circumstances attendant with creation: the earth was formless and desolate, darkness was upon the face of the abyss, and God's Spirit was hovering over the surface of the waters. What does this mean and at what time did all this happen?

An earth "without form and void" is to be understood primarily in terms of God's ultimate intention for the earth. That is, as Genesis goes on to explain, the earth, in response to God's direction, takes on orderly features and is made the place for man to dwell (cf. Isaiah 45:18). Genesis 1:2 does not mean that God created a chaos; it rather describes that at that time it was not yet ready for man. The "abyss" refers to the primeval waters, and it is the assertion of Genesis that even here God's Spirit was in control. "Spirit" might also be rendered "wind" or "breath," but the emphasis throughout this section on what God does argues to the contrary. In this creation account of thirty-four verses the word "God" occurs thirty five-times.

How long a period of time is involved in Genesis 1:2? Perhaps years, perhaps days, or perhaps no more than moments. The text does not say. The well-known Scottish preacher Thomas Chalmers (1780-1847) argued from this verse that over long eons of time the earth "became" formless and void, and that from such a chaos God reconstructed or reconstituted the earth in six days of creation. Chalmers was followed by C.J.Schofield who incorporated these views into his annotated Bible. Apparently his theory was to bring about harmony between Genesis and geology on the age of the earth; and because it demanded a long "gap" of time between verses 1 and 2, it is generally known as "the gap theory." But it is important to recognize that the text of Genesis gives no clue whatever to the extent of time covered in verse 2. Days or ages are presupposed in this verse, or rather are imposed on the verse in league with a particular theory of interpretation. Elsewhere Scripture gives no support for a reconstitution theory, and the theory runs aground in Genesis 1:14-19.

GENESIS 1:3

The first day of the creation week begins with the Divine declaration, "Let there be light." This light is not an emanation from God, it is a creation of the Divine Word. "He spoke, and it came to be" (Psalm 33:9). Light before the sun is a specific intentional detail of Genesis on origins. Common knowledge, of course, would associate light with the sun, but the author of Genesis lays stress on God and not the sun as the Source of light. Light is the prime essential for life on earth, and so light is the first thing mentioned as created.

With the second and third days, attention is directed to the appearance of earth and the beginning of all plant life. God's commanding the earth to bring forth vegetation makes it clear that life cannot arise apart from God, nor can the earth of itself produce life. That this occurs on the third day, before the making of the sun on the fourth day, is once again an intentional detail of Genesis. Trees and plants have their life in God and did exist apart from the sun as it is now known.

The fourth day of creation is marked by the Divine calling of lights in the expanse of the sky. How is this to be understood? If, as is likely, Genesis 1:1 is to be taken as an independent clause, an absolute statement that God made everything in the beginning, then the heavenly bodies were made to exist from the beginning and on the fourth day they are established as lights to give light on the earth. Indeed, the Genesis text says that they were set for signs and seasons, and for days and years. The emphasis is on their function and for their serving as lights for earth.

With the fifth and sixth days, the waters swarm with living things, the birds fly across the sky, and the earth brings forth living creatures of cattle, reptiles, and wild animals. This is done, to be sure, by God's power, for it is prefaced by, "And God said." (Eight distinct times Genesis 1 relates, "And God said.") It is pointedly stated, as earlier references to plant life, that all living things bear each "according to its kind." Each has its distinction and is to preserve its distinctiveness.

The climax of creation is the making of man, male and female. Although earlier it is said that the waters and earth bring forth living things, it is noticeable that the text does not now read, "Let the earth bring forth man." To the contrary, man's creation is especially significant: God deliberates with Himself concerning the creation of man and decides that man is to be made in His own image. In context, man in the likeness of God means that man, like the Creator, is to have dominion — in man's case over the whole earth and all living things.

The week of creation is concluded with God's taking rest on the seventh day. This was not a rest of exhaustion but of satisfying fulfillment which accompanies a finished task.

Although the Genesis account gives a number of details with reference to creation, a number of others are omitted. Nothing, for instance, is said about angels, about Satan, or about the origin of evil. Many questions are left unanswered. In Genesis 1 there is a kind of outline of what transpired, a summation of the main events in the earliest dawning of history. Yet logical order and arrangement persist throughout: the formless, then the formed, light before life, plants before animals, animals before man, man both male and female. And there is a chronological sequence that cannot be compromised. Evening and morning comprise a day, and there is a first day, a second day, a third day and so on until in six days God has made a world for man and fit for his rule.

SPECIAL POINTS OF EMPHASIS

Looking back over the Genesis account of creation, certain truths stand out prominently and require special consideration:

1. *In the beginning God created matter.* The late Professor Harlow Shapley of Harvard University used to state: "Some people piously proclaim, 'In the beginning, God.' I say, 'In the beginning hydrogen.'" Shapley believed that starting with hydrogen, and given sufficient lengths of time, he could explain the origin of everthing. He could, of course, do no such thing, but at least his claims were consistent with his atheistic philosophy.

Numerous hypotheses have been advanced in recent years to explain the origin of our solar system. But bold and ingenious hypotheses, whether in the form of continuous creation, or a "big bang" explosion of protons and neutrons, or an accidental cosmic collision, cannot account for the present condition of the solar system, much less the existence of the "raw material" out of which it is made. Strictly speaking, either matter is eternal and somehow sustains its own existence, or else God is eternal and is the source of all material things. Scripture affirms the latter. Apart from Scripture, from the standpoint of reason alone, creation by an omnipotent God remains a logical hypothesis to explain the origin of the universe.

2. *In the beginning God created life.* Multiform theories also have been set forth in an attempt to describe how life might have arisen by chance. One theory argued for in an article in *Science* (Vol. 131, p.1519) is particularly interesting, given all of its "givens." The author of the article liked the idea "where local conditions of heat and pressure could have reduced the carbon, where phosphorus was abundant, where potassium predominates over sodium, where the ammonia produced by lightning could collect, and where the preliving organic soup could be concentrated easily by a little evaporation . . . . that life started on the surface of quartz particles in a pond on the south side of a volcano (in the Northern Hemisphere, of course)."

With an abundance of such vapid theories extant, it is not surprising that two British scientists have recently reversed their views and have become advocates of a supernatural creation. The two scientists are well-known, Sir Fred Hoyle, mathematician and astronomer of Cambridge; and Chadra Wickramasinghe, astronomer and mathematician at University College, Cardiff, Wales. Based on their knowledge of the minimum requirements of a cell, and working independently of each other, they calculated the probability of life evolving on earth over a period of five billion years. The probability of such turned out to be one chance out of $10^{40,000}$ — that is, one chance out of 1 followed by 40,000 zeros.

Hoyle and Wickramasinghe further calculated the probability of life evolving anywhere in the universe. Assuming that the universe is composed of 100 billion galaxies of 100 billion stars each, that each star has a planet like the earth, and that the universe is 20 billion years old — again, the probability was practically zero.

Hoyle has gone so far as to maintain that an evolutionary origin of life is equal to the probability that a tornado,

sweeping through a junkyard, could assemble a Boeing 747. The report of this story appeared in the London *Daily Express,* August 14, 1981, with the headlines: "Two skeptical scientists put their heads together and reach an amazing conclusion: THERE MUST BE A GOD."
It needs to be understood clearly that these two scientists are not believers in the Bible, but nevertheless they have concluded that the existence of life in the universe requires a supernatural act of creation.

3. *In the beginning God created life after its kind.* According to Genesis, God is the source of life in general and life in specific forms. Nine different times the text affirms that God made things "after their kinds." The scientific law, that "like begets like," is an unvarying experience of life. According to naturalistic evolution, like must beget unlike. The same holds true for various theories of theistic evolution. The Genesis creation account, according to which things increase "after their kinds," does not leave room for any view where God did his work of creation by means of evolution.

The term for "kind" is the Hebrew word *min,* which basically denotes a "split" or "division." In the Old Testament *min* is applied only to living things and usually to animal life. Genesis 1:21 uses *min* in connection with broad groups of water creatures and birds; Genesis 1:24,25 relates *min* to the broad categories of cattle, reptiles, and wild animals. In other passages, however, *min* is used to refer to specific kinds of birds (Lev. 11:13-19) and to specific kinds of edible locusts (Lev. 11:22). It is obvious, therefore, that *min* does not correspond in usage with the nomenclature of biologists of today. *Min* is not the exact equivalent of the modern term "specie."

According to Genesis, things brought forth in their own divisions or groups. It may be that within these groups there may have been considerable development over a period of time. *This is where practically all of the evidence for evolution applies.* If it is granted, for instance, that the modern horse has developed through the stages of Eohippus, Mesohippus, and

Protohippus, *this still is not in conflict with Genesis.* Scripture affirms that God made things in their own groups; and evolution, on a grand scale, has not begun to prove its case until it can produce evidence for transition from one major group into another major group.

4. *In the beginning God created male and female.* There are several lines of evidence from Scripture which show that human beings are a special creation of God. (1) Man is made in the image of God. Human beings, therefore, did not evolve from animals which are not made in God's image. (2) Genesis 2:7 states that man became a living person when God breathed life into him. Man did not exist prior to this, which means that he is not a descendant of some other form of life. (3) Scripture clearly states that man and woman are separate creations by God. God made Adam as the first man, and God made Eve from Adam. No evolutionary hypothesis can make sense out of this or can be compatible with this. Man, according to Genesis, is a miracle, God's unique creation, genetically unconnected with any form of existing life.

THE MEANING OF "DAY"

The creation account in Genesis is placed within a definite chronological scheme. Specific acts of creation are associated with specific days, and everything was made in six days. What is the meaning of the word "day," and how much time can be allowed for in these creation days?

The Hebrew word for day is *yom,* which in Scripture can mean not only "day" but "time", "life," "age," "forever," and so forth. What is important here, however, is not the meanings *yom* may have, but the meaning it does have in this particular context of Genesis.

A good case can be made for *yom* in Genesis 1 as a twenty-four hour solar day. (1) This is the ordinary meaning of "day" and what one would normally think of in reading a sequence of days, such as "first day," "second day," "third day," and so on. (2) The text defines and limits "day" with the expression "evening and morning," which suggests a solar day. (3) Exodus 20:11 says that "in six days the Lord made heaven and earth, the sea, and all that is in them, and rested the seventh day." In this verse the six days of creation are made to correspond to the six days of the week when man is to do his work. Therefore, it would appear that the days of creation are solar days.

On the other hand, it is possible that Genesis attaches a different sense to *yom*. Indeed, *yom* seems to have several meanings in the course of the Genesis creation account: (1) In Genesis 1:5 the word "day" is used for "daytime," the opposite of night, and also for "one day," including evening and morning. (2) In Genesis 1:5,8,13 "day," referring to the first three days, may stand for something other than a twenty-four hour solar day. The sun, and perhaps the solar system as it now is, were not made "for seasons and for days and years" until the fourth day. If the standard by which days are now measured was not created until the fourth day, how can the first three days be precisely defined as solar days? In the strictest sense, until day four, there were no solar days. (3) In Genesis 2:4 the word "day" includes all of the "days" of creation. (4) Combining Genesis chapter 1 and chapter 2 may indicate that the sixth day of creation was longer than twenty-four hours.. On the sixth day God creates Adam; Adam names "every living creature" and yet fails to find a companion for himself; God creates Eve and presents her to Adam; and Adam exclaims, "This at last . . . ."

What, then, is the meaning of *yom* in the creation account? Obviously, this is not a simple question with a clear-cut answer. One suspects that the Genesis account of creation was not originally written to bring before the reader's mind unusual complexities and subtleties from a "modern science" point of view. Certainly if "day" in Genesis refers to an "age" or "ages" of time, this may help in some respects but in other respects it raises many more and greater problems. One is left with the impression that the most natural way to understand the six days of creation is to think of them in terms of six days that approximate six twenty-four hour days. But here dogmatism is not only unwise but is actually *unscriptural!*

AGE OF THE EARTH AND OF MAN

Everyone agrees that naturalistic evolution requires an immense span of time spread out hundreds of millions of years. Is this possible? How old is the earth? And how long has man been on earth? What does the Bible teach on these questions?

Science generally posits an old earth — the earth whose age is perhaps four or five billion years or more, the universe with an estimated age of some fifteen to twenty billion years. Some scientists, however, argue for a young earth, which dates to 10,000 years or so.

It is important to emphasize that the Bible does not declare itself on the age of the earth. For the Christian this is no more than an incidental item of interest. When was "in the beginning?" How long was the earth formless and unpopulated, before God said, "Let there be light?" Scripture simply does not deal with these questions.

How long man has been on the earth is a different matter. In Genesis and elsewhere the Bible states that Adam was the first man (1 Tim.2:13; 1 Chron. 1:1; Luke 3:38; cf. Matt.19:4; Rom. 5:12-14; 1 Cor. 15:21,22). What about fossil man? From the vantage point of Scripture, when fossils are found — if they are truly human — they must be descendants of Adam. The Bible knows nothing of pre-Adamites.

173

It is at this point that problems emerge, for how can fossil man be dated hundreds of thousands of years ago and the Bible teach that man has been on the earth only about 6,000 years? Of course, the question in this form cannot be responded to, because it assumes what is contrary to fact. On one hand, the dating of human remains into hundreds of thousands of years is controversial and is therefore part of the problem. On the other hand, the Bible offers no evidence by which to determine the time of Adam's creation.

The Bible does not hold that man has been on earth only about 6,000 years. This view, instead of coming from the Bible, is due to Archbishop James Ussher of the Church of England in the seventeenth century. Ussher, on the basis of the genealogies and other chronological data in Scripture, worked out a time-chart that placed the creation of man in the year 4004 B.C. John Lightfoot of Cambridge later went so far as to say that Adam was created on October 23, 4004 B.C., at 9:00 a.m., forty-fifth meridian time. One acute writer has suggested that beyond that, Lightfoot, as a cautious scholar, would not commit himself. But it is important to remember that any such dating does not rest on the Bible, but on Ussher's interpretations of Biblical chronology.

Ussher's system of chronology is based on several questionable assumptions. First, it assumes that the dates throughout the Old Testament should be followed as preserved in the Massoretic Text (standard Hebrew text). However, many dates in the Septuagint (the Greek translation of the Old Testament) and the Samaritan Pentateuch differ from those in the Massoretic Text. The Septuagint, for example, lengthens the period of time from Adam to Abraham by more than 1300 years. It may be that the Hebrew text is more exact, but Ussher's system depends upon the meticulous accuracy of the Hebrew text at precisely all of the points where there are differences.

Second, Ussher's system assumes that the early genealogies in Genesis 5 and 11 are successive generations from father to son. This a large assumption, for not infrequently in the Old Testament "son of," "father of," and "begat" indicate a broad relationship. In Genesis 46:21 the "sons of Benjamin" include grandsons as well as sons; in Matthew 1:1 Jesus is described as "the son of David, the son of Abraham." So a genealogical table in Scripture might denote something other than a strict father-son relationship.

Third, Ussher's system assumes that the author of Genesis sought to record a complete, detailed genealogy back to the time of Adam. But it may well be that Genesis is concerned only with the main line of descent. This is Matthew's interest in the most important of genealogies, that of Jesus Christ. Matthew did not give a full genealogy. He omitted three generations after Joram in order that in his list there might be the symmetry of fourteen generations, separating the main periods of Jewish history. If Matthew's genealogy is abbreviated, it is also quite possible that the genealogies in Genesis are also abbreviated. A careful study of the ages of the patriarchs give hints that the genealogies in Genesis are not complete. Otherwise Noah, Shem, Arpachshad, Shelah, Eber, and Peleg would all be contemporaries of Abraham, and Shem, the son of Noah, would still be living at the time of Jacob's birth. What seems to be intended here, therefore, is not a complete chronology but only the tracing of the main genealogical tree.

How long has man lived on the earth? Hundreds of thousands, or perhaps millions of years? This is not likely. The Old Testament genealogies may not be complete, but surely they are not to be stretched out to the point that they would have little meaning. This would be the case if man has been on earth hundreds of thousands of years, and possibly millions of years. Further, as one looks at the text of Genesis, chapters 3 and 4 are closely linked. Both chapters make reference to Adam and

Eve, but chapter four also mentions such things as city building, musical instruments and tools of bronze and iron. In other words, Genesis directly connects civilization with early man. If men were on earth hundreds of thousands of years ago, what were they doing? Archaeologists speak of various civilizations around 10,000 or so years ago, but not in terms of hundreds of thousands of years.

CONCLUDING OBSERVATIONS

1. *The Genesis account of creation gives a summary of what God said and did in His acts of creation.* The emphasis throughout is on God's speaking, on God's commands, and on God's approval of what was done. In this way the reader of Genesis is introduced to the most important Fact and Power and Person in the universe — God Himself. God is the One Being behind it all, without Whom no thing is.

2. *The Genesis account, though in two parts (chapters 1 and 2), is nevertheless but one account of creation.* Chapter 1 provides the general framework of the creation narrative, while chapter 2 adds specifics on the creation of man, the creation of woman, the garden of Eden and its location, and so forth. Chapter 2 is not contradictory to chapter 1 but presupposes chapter 1 and prepares for what follows in chapter 3.

3. *There are, indeed, parallels that can be drawn between the Genesis account of creation and various Near-Eastern mythological creation stories.* That which by far has more affinities with Genesis than any other is the Babylonian-Assyrian epic poem known as *Enuma Elish* ("When above," the opening words of the poem). But the differences between *Enuma Elish* and Genesis are many and major. The classic work on this is Alexander Heidel's *The Babylonian Genesis.* Heidel's painstaking study on the whole problem should be read. Comparing *Enuma Elish* and Genesis, Heidel stresses the *differences*

between the two, in the light of which, he says, "the resemblances fade away almost like the stars before the sun" (p. 139).

4. *Macro-evolution, by which the origin of everything is supposed to be explained, is the "grand myth" of modern times.* ("Grand myth" was C.S. Lewis' expression for the all-encompassing hypothesis of evolution.) Darwin's *Origin of the Species* was but one long argument for evolution, it was not a *demonstration* of evolution. Certainly Darwin did not show *how* evolution occurred. The mechanism, the machinery by which it all happened, is still significantly absent in the latest evolutionary theories.

5. *It is not anti-intellectual or naive or obscurantist to believe that a Supreme Creator is responsible for the high degree of order present in the universe.* Nor is it, for that matter, naive to believe that the opening chapters of Genesis are a *revelation* from the Creator. Whoever the author of Genesis was — Moses? — he could not have carefully investigated or employed reliably traditional sources of information accessible to him on the days of creation. No human witness was present during those creation days. God alone through His speaking gives correct information on the week of creation. (Is it really naive to believe that God spoke to Moses?) This is implicit in these early chapters of Genesis, just as it is explicit later in Genesis that God spoke to men such as Noah, Abraham, and Joseph.

The Genesis account of creation, therefore, should be read for what it purports to be: a straightforward, sober statement of what actually happened. The whole Book of Genesis claims to be historical, and its opening chapters on creation are an integral part of Genesis' uncompromising historical character.

12

EVOLUTION AND FAITH

J. D. THOMAS

We have come a long way in our study of evolution and its relation to faith. We have seen that not only does the theory relate to Christian faith, but that its acceptance also requires a faith on the part of those who believe in evolution. It lacks demonstrability, which means that it cannot ever be called a scientific fact, and that it must always remain in the realm of loose science. It is really a conclusion based on the philosophy of scientism. It is as much a faith as creation is a faith. Neither conclusion has or even can have "hard fact" scientific proof. One's personal faith should seek to determine which is the more reasonable faith, based on the totality of facts that are available. Much prejudice has been expressed on both sides of the issue, even in the courts of our land, so each person should strive to rise above mere prejudice and learn the real facts for himself.

In this chapter we consider further some of the teachings of the Bible. There have been abuses of the teachings of scripture as well as abuses of the facts of science. It is just as wrong to try to bind upon people an incorrect teaching of scripture as it is any other incorrect doctrine. Truth requires unbiased searching upon the part of each one of us, but true faith can be obtained.

AGE OF THE UNIVERSE AND THE EARTH

In chapter 9 we promised that in the Bible section of the book we would discuss in some detail Problem No.13 of those which were first listed in the Introduction chapter — *The Biblical demands — What the Bible actually says concerning the Age of the Earth and of Man; about the Flood; about "kinds" of creatures and the possibility of changes in life forms.* Dr. Lightfoot has ably treated much of this material in his discussion of The *Week of Creation* (Chapter 11), but since these questions are troubling so many people we comment on them even further.

What does the Bible say as to the age of the universe and of the earth? In Genesis 1:1 we have the statement, "In the beginning God created the heavens and the earth," but there is no time reference given in this verse to which the original creation can be related, no way to tell how long ago this occurred. It could have been recent, but it also could have been a long time ago. We would note that if a person should believe in a very old universe and earth, this does not require that he also accepts uniformitarianism as the correct geological philosophy. He can still believe that there was a creation. Both "young earth" and "old earth" adherents are among those who believe in what Genesis actually teaches about fiat creation.

Verse 2 next says, "The earth was without form and void, and darkness was upon the face of the deep; and the Spirit of God was moving over the face of the waters." Again there is no time reference nor indication as to how long this "without form and void" condition lasted. This chaotic condition, whereof all created matter remained in a disorganized state, could have lasted for a long time, or, for only a short time. We note also that this condition existed before the "days of creation" began. So, there is no definite time period to apply to the original beginning.

Some interpreters argue that there was an original orderly creation, which later "became" chaotic or in the "without form and void" state noted above. The argument here is that the "was" of verse two really should be translated "became," so that there was a "gap" or orderly period which became chaotic and then was reconstructed or restored to orderliness during the "days" of creation. This argument is based on the fact that "was" and "became" are logically close meanings of the same root word, "to be." "Was" indicates being in a state of being, and "became" means the entering of that state of being, so that the meanings are interchangeable, and this is true in both Hebrew and Greek, as well as English. If this Gap-theory be true, then there would be ample time for any fossils to be fitted in.

Another theory that is offered to show that the Bible does not require a 6,000 year old universe and earth is that the "days" of the creation period could each be a long period of time. The Hebrew word *yom* does have several different meanings in the scriptures, as Dr. Lightfoot has noted. The King James Bible translates *yom* as "age" six different times among the other meanings it gives. To carry this argument to its conclusion means that it is possible that the earth was very old when man arrived on the scene.

The above brief arguments each have some possibilities, yet each of them also has weaknesses and problems. This writer realizes that we simply do not yet know what the full facts are and therefore cannot either endorse or deny any of them at this stage of our knowledge. We can agree, however, that the Bible does not make any definite requirements about what we believe about a date that should be assigned to the creation, or the beginning of "the heavens and the earth." Whether 6,000 years or billions of years as the age of the universe and the earth be one's personal belief, his reasons for such a faith obviously do not come from the Bible but from some external source.

We must remember Dr. Fair's admonition that the Bible is not a science textbook, and we must not expect it to provide scientific details. We have the fact of God's creation clearly taught, which meets the religious purpose, and that is as much detail as we need for a full and valid faith.

THE ANTIQUITY OF MAN

Archbishop Ussher, who was head of the Church of England in the seventeenth century, is the one responsible for the idea of the 6,000 year age of the earth since the creation. Ussher dated the creation at 4004 B.C. and as Archbishop, he influenced the printers of the new King James Bible to print his figures in the margin of Genesis one, the result of which was that many ordinary persons came to believe that his figures were also scripture. He had arrived at his date of 4004 by adding up the ages of the patriarchs in Genesis chapters 5 and 11, while assuming that the genealological lists were also exact chronological lists. (A genealogy serves to indicate a line of descent, while a chronology serves to indicate the amounts of time involved). Ussher also assumed that the Massoretic (Hebrew language) text of Genesis was the original one and that the numbers we have in the King James Bible are all correct. All of these assumptions are open to question, and we know for sure that the genealogies cannot serve as exact end-to-end chronologies, because if so they would disagree with other chronological statements in scripture, and this would result in some very strange date relationships and overlappings.

For instance, Dr. W.H. Green has observed that Moses' grandson would have been living in David's day; his grandfather would have had 8,600 male descendants during Moses' day; and a great grandson and the grandson of Aaron together with a son of David would have been among the number returning with Ezra from Babylon about 430-450 B.C. Names are omitted from some genealogical lists; "beget" can refer to grandsons and others in the posterity besides sons; brothers are listed as descendants and in Genesis 36:11,12 a concubine is listed among sons. (See "Primeval Chronology" in *Bibliotheca Sacra*, 1890, pp.285-303; Also discussed in my *Facts and Faith*, Vol. I, pp.166-172).

Biblical chronology is fairly definite and fairly certain from Abraham's date on down to us, but it is very indefinite from Abraham back to Adam. The lines of descent are dependable, but the chronology is recognized by all as not being exact or definite. Surely it would be wrong to make any date for Adam a test of faith.

What all the above means is that not only the Bible does not make any definite statement about the age of the earth, but it does not limit us to any certain date for Adam. We may believe what we desire to believe, but we do not have Bible authority for any certain date.

RECENCY OF MAN

Although we have been insisting that the Bible does not demand any certain age for man on the earth, we still say that there is excellent scientific evidence for the recency of his arrival.

Genesis 4 indicates a high degree of tool-making, agriculture and music. We have no evidence of any civilization earlier than 6000 to 7000 B.C. (There have been some recent claims for life in Amercia that reach back a few thousand years earlier than this). But as noted in Chapter 9, people apparently quit living in caves about 5000 B.C., and our first known city was at Jericho in Palestine about that time. The small-stone tools that were used in the last cave dwellings in Palestine are similar to those used in the first city occupation. Many of us probably think of cave-dwelling as something that happened eons ago, but we should realize that it does not go back very far. In fact, it is still going on in some places of the world, notably among the Australian Aborigines.

The dating of ancient man, based on findings in geology and paleontology is still strongly suspect. The use of radioactive dating techniques on human remains is also questionable, since bones do not have enough carbon in them for accurate testing and there are no soft parts left. Radioactive testing, therefore, must be done on lava or something found near the fossil remains, and then one has to assume an accurate relationship between the objects and the bones.

If we will keep in mind the purpose of the Bible — that it was written for religious ends rather than for scientific or even chronological purposes, we will relieve it from the considerable pressures that some have been prone to place upon it. There is certainly no contradiction between any properly interpreted Biblical statement and any "hard fact" that has been discovered by science.

THE GENESIS FLOOD

As with other matters we are discussing, we lack strict science proof for questions about the flood, on both sides of the issues. We can't prove that there was such a flood, and it cannot be proved that it did not occur. Whatever one believes, he does so on the basis of faith, not facts that can be demonstrated. This probably explains the many efforts over recent years to find Noah's ark on Mount Ararat.

Concerning the flood, first of all is the clash between naturalism and supernaturalism as the basic philosophical approach to all religious matters. The naturalists usually insist that all the first eleven chapters of Genesis are mere legend and are adaptations of pagan myths that were in circulation. The article "Deluge" in the Encyclopedia Biblica gives a somewhat standard critical view, under the assumption that the Genesis flood story is folklore and unhistorical.

The naturalism-supernaturalism clash is also seen in the theories of geology that are adopted concerning the flood, with neither side being able to furnish clear-cut proof. Extreme supernaturalists tend to insist on geological catastrophes, with the flood as the best illustration, being responsible for depositing the various rock strata and fossils that now exist. A problem with this is that many strata and fossil deposits date in different periods with some going back farther than any reasonable date for the flood, which must necessarily be after man had been here for some time.

Radical naturalists, on the other hand, take as their chief hypothesis Lyell's Uniformitarianism theory and try to force everything into that mold, not allowing for any significant catastrophes that might have had any major geological impact. Their uniformity doctrine insists that "the present is the key to the past."

The trouble is that each camp of flood theorists seem to err to the extreme. The uniformitarians "date the rocks by the fossils and the fossils by the rocks"; while those who champion catastrophism want to have flood-geology do more than it could possibly do, since both rock and fossil formations differ in age and one flood could not explain all.

There are differences also among those who believe in the Genesis flood. Some want it to be a universal flood while others say it was merely local, geographically and/or anthropologically. These points and others have been suggested and argued through the years without much success, so that there is no simple explanation on the part of those who believe in the flood.

The several large fossil deposits and numerous catastrophic upheavals mentioned by Dr. Felix in chapter 3 prove to be "thorns in the flesh" to the uniformitarians and seem to be beyond explanation by them. They also have to assume that their "uniformitarianism" provides a constant rate of change throughout time, which in view of all of the known catastrophes seems impossible.

It is no problem to believe in the Genesis flood if one is a man of faith. No fact is known that can deny it as a real event. But since it cannot be proved conclusively, we cannot force its acceptance on the opposition. Like most of the rest of the Bible, we are left to the realm of faith. Faith is quite reasonable in the total outlook, but it must remain faith. Christianity is a faith religion, by plan.

THEISTIC EVOLUTION

Theistic evolution, or "religious evolution," is the effort on the part of some people of faith to compromise with atheistic evolution. They want to be truly religious but they fear that there must be something to evolution (macro-) since so many people accept it, and they do not want to be found rejecting any truth. So, they say, maybe God used evolution as his method of creation. Good Christians and even some preachers are caught up in this attitude, which does, after all, reflect little knowledge of the real issues.

There are three choices: 1) Fiat creation, where God spoke things into existence ; 2) Atheistic evolution which takes

Naturalism as its basic philosophy and accepts a "chance" and "mindless" view of origins; and, 3) Theistic evolution, where it is felt that God somehow did create but that evolution is also, somehow true. Actually theistic evolution was invented to bridge the gap and make a compromise between Christian faith and naturalistic evolution. Technically, the human body and the life forms of animals came about through the action of natural law only. At some proper point God, by fiat creation, infused man's animal body with a human soul or spirit, at which time man became a real, complete human.

Some major religious groups today hold for some form of theistic evolution, and this includes some conservative groups and some professors in conservative seminaries. These facts make it somewhat easy for laymen to also make the compromise. Question: Is the compromise justified or necessary?

The real problem is, whether atheistic evolution has been proved. If not, there is no reason to question fiat creation in the first place. The issue is, did all the known forms of life develop into their present major classifications and minor classifications from one or a few original molecules or even "naked genes?" We are not now dealing with "differentiation" or "speciation," but with what is macro-evolution with a vengeance. Remember that there is no evidence whatever that any member of one phylum ever had an ancestor in another phylum. This fact alone destroys the theory, when one thinks it through. Known changes, as speciation, or variations, do not explain or justify the doctrine of macro-evolution. No doubt that all dogs came from one original pair. All people came from Adam and Eve. But this is simply change, not macro-evolution.

There is no reason to compromise with an unreasonable theory or with a mathematical improbability. There is no need to accept the crossing of phyla, which macro-evolution would demand, when none has ever been known! Why should Christians believe in spontaneous generation of life, when it is contrary to scientific law? Why should believers in creation assume that all the gaps in the fossil record have been filled in and made complete, when this is a far cry from the truth? Why should Christians assume a mechanism for naturalistic evolution, when 125 years of heavy efforts have failed to find one?

We conclude that there is no basis for compromising with atheistic evolution and therefore no place for a doctrine of theistic evolution.

13

THE PRESENT PICTURE

J. D. THOMAS

W e have about come to the end of our study together, with the exception of some summary thoughts which may help individuals in reaching their conclusions and commitments. Surely there is "a great cloud of witnesses" for each of the several views discussed, and we realize that there is no such thing as a consensus of agreement, since there are "smart people" on each side of the several issues. Each of us must study for ourselves and then commit to whatever we can live with in good conscience.

Let us bring into sharp focus the major conclusions:

SUMMARY FROM SCIENCE

The Expanding Universe, which is a demonstrable scientific fact, suggests that there was *a beginning* of all things, and the fact of a beginning is accepted now by most scientists, whereas evolutionists used to argue that "the universe has always been."

The beginning was in both space and time, so that at the very first both matter and energy were located in a compact situation. The beginning has been called the "Big Bang," at the time of which "explosion" the expansion of the universe began. The fact of a beginning agrees with the creation outlook.

Micro-evolution, which is the same as "change," "variation," "differentiation," and "speciation," is a demonstrable, scientific fact, as has been shown in several of the articles in this book. There is no question but that such changes do occur, and that they can be hereditary. Although all human beings are derived from Adam and Eve, we are divided into races, with different colors of skin, different tendencies to height, different facial expressions, and other distinguishing characteristics, all of which are hereditary. But all of this is in the category of minor changes, compared to what would be required if "amoeba-to-man," macro-evolution, were true. There simply is no evidence for the latter, and the belief that it is true, therefore, has to be assumed. It is "extrapolated," from what occurs in the minor divisions of taxonomy to the major divisions, and, since there is not nor ever has been any physical evidence to support changes from one phylum to another, we have to admit that the theory of evolution is but a faith, and is not a scientific fact.

Intense searching for evidence for "gradual" evolution has gone on since Darwin's day. What has been found is rather the "sudden" appearance of new types of life forms, fully developed, and with no indication that they came from previous forms. Leading scientists of today (e.g., S.J.Gould of Harvard) who hold to evolution, have therefore now given up Darwin's idea of gradualism and admit to the fact of sudden emergence of new forms, calling it "Punctuated Equilibrium" or some such designation. The fact is that even back from the late PreCambrian period, when the first fossils appear, we have fully developed phyla that have continued right on into the present day without change. This means that the idea that got all the

"Evolution argument" started, Darwin's belief in gradualism (with all the time available that could ever be needed), is no longer believed by the evolutionists, and the time factor no longer obtains since a "beginning" is now accepted. This means that people still insist on believing in evolution although they have changed their reasoning why. Apparently they now believe in it purely for emotional reasons rather than because "science has proved it." Certain proof is still lacking, even in the slightest degree.

Throughout the century and a quarter since Darwin, fossils have been admitted to be the strongest, and really, the only absolute proof that could justify faith in evolution. So, fossil arrangements have been artistically designed for the museums. They do not represent actual fossil hoards but are only artificial constructions. Actually fossils that might contribute anything have proved to be both very scarce and very incomplete. Note the following from Oswald Spengler, noted German scholar:

> There is no more conclusive refutation of Darwinism than that furnished by paleontology. Simple probability indicates that fossil hoards can only be test samples. Each sample, then, would represent a different stage of evolution, and there ought to be merely "transitional" types, no definition and no species. Instead of this we find perfectly stable and and unaltered forms persevering through long ages, forms that have not developed themselves on the fitness principle, but appear suddenly and at once in their definitive shape; that do not thereafter evolve towards better adaptation, but become rarer and finally disappear, while quite different forms crop up again. What unfolds itself, in ever increasing richness of form, is the great classes and kinds of living beings which existed aboriginally and exist still, without transition types, in the grouping of today.[1]

SUMMARY FROM THE BIBLE

As we look at the Bible and particularly the creation account in Genesis, with respect to what might be learned relative to the claims made for evolution, we are conscious that the Bible has made no statements that bear upon the age of the universe or of the earth. As far as the Biblical text is concerned, the language used has simply not committed itself to any date for the creation. Further, 2 Peter 3:8 states that "with the Lord one day is as a thousand years, and a thousand years as one day." This means that time is not a problem nor is it a factor with God's planning and working.

Neither does the Bible make any requirement as to when we date Adam, the first man. There is simply no way to determine how long Adam preceded Abraham, with whom relatively certain dating began. The listings of the patriarchs and their genealogies found in Genesis were given for purposes of genealogy, not chronology, and there is enough variation in them to know for sure that they do not furnish absolute chronological information.

GENESIS AND MYTH

Many scholars who are under the influence of Naturalistic philosophy believe that Genesis is not a literal account of how the original world, and Adam and Eve, came to be, but that it has only a "mythical" meaning, and we therefore can dismiss any literal interpretation. By "myth" it is felt that the account is fabulous and unhistorical, filled with non-literal language, and that it was given only to advance a tradition.

In scripture there should be some reason given why a passage is to be understood as non-literal if that be the case, and in figurative speech each figure has a meaning, even though it be non-literal. There should be a counterpart literal reality for each part of the figurative representation. With this understanding, the creation account in Genesis tells of Adam's becoming "a livng soul" and then we are told about Eve being formed from a rib taken from Adam's side, to become his helpmate and to become the mother of all living. The point here is that the "rib story" has no literal counterpart, if this is only a mythical tale. The rib story doesn't correspond to any point of literal truth if it is only a figure of speech, whereas the other parts of the account would have a counterpart. Actually, in the evolution view, you have both male and female members of the species on hand long before man became a living soul. We conclude, therefore, that Eve was *literally* formed from Adam's body, and since man is normally born of woman, this means that man and woman are dependent upon each other for their very existence, as 1 Corinthians 11:8,9 indicates.

Again, the "mythical" interpreters have no explanation for Adam's sin and "fall;" neither for the statements that one pair of human beings are the parents of all humanity. Apparently the trouble is that the naturalistic interpreters do not want to admit the existence of God. If God is, then there is no problem to any of the material in Genesis chapters 1-11 (that which covers the history before Abraham).

The great danger to all this discussion is that people form decisions and make conclusions without knowing what the facts really are. Ignorance of these details is found among the intelligentsia as well as those less well educated.

ASSUMPTIONS OF EVOLUTIONISTS

A major assumption of those who accept macro-evolution is the philosophy of Naturalism. This view is best contrasted with Supernaturalism, of which it is the diametrical opposite. It assumes that Nature is the whole of reality and that all problems can be answered from within the physical realm rather than giving any consideration to a metaphysical or supernatural realm. To illustrate that evolutionists tend to assume Naturalism as their basic philosophy we quote the following:

> We must attack from the naturalistic point of view; namely, that principles unknown or unknowable to science cannot be used to solve the problem. In other words, we proceed under the assumption that

life is a process that escapes at present our complete understanding, only for the reason of its complexity.[2] It is, however, an obvious lesson from the history of scientific progress that in science one should never accept a metaphysical explanation if a physical explanation is possible, or, indeed, conceivable.[3]

The above quotations reflect a confidence that though science hasn't yet solved all the "complexity" that it does hold the key and has the perfect methodology for getting at all truth, even any truth that might be in a non-physical realm of reality.

It is our observation that such confidence is unjustified. The realm of values, spiritual realities, and of abstract ideas is very important to man's well-being and purposes; and the average man of the street believes that these things are very real. Since science is limited to the physical realm, there is much of true reality that it can never know.

A second major assumption of the evolutionists is that of *extrapolation* of the evidence, of change from what really does occur among the minor groups of the taxa, to what is not known to occur among the major groupings, such as Phyla, Classes and Orders. We do not deny that sometimes extrapolation is justifiable, but there must be a reason why, and if evolution were the true logical conclusion we should have all manner of evidence in the form of transitional fossils (See Spengler's comment above, Note 1).

A third major assumption that seems completely unjustified is that of "Chance probabilities," that our marvelous universe and world were formed by natural actions without the influence of a guiding mind. For example, every part in the human body, seems to "dovetail" or integrate well with the other parts in the body. The eye itself is such a remarkable instrument that logic would require a designer instead of thinking that it could just evolve itself. Evolutionists themselves admit that the mathematical improbabilities of evolution are so great that it is an impossibility (See Huxley's quotation, Note 6 in Chapter 9).

There are numerous other unjustified assumptions in the philosophy of evolution but the three given above illustrate the argument well, and any one of them is of sufficient import to destroy the viability of the theory.

UNSOLVED PROBLEMS OF EVOLUTIONISTS

In summarizing we list again some of the unsolved problems that need to be explained before evolution could be believed:

1) The earth and the universe had a beginning; they have not "always been."

2) There is an absence of data about a *beginning of life* on earth.

3) There is an absence of data about development from the first spark of life up to the first protozoa, or fossil form.

4) The sudden appearance of the various forms of life, as the fossils indicate, with no indication of relation to any previous forms.

5) The fact that many fully formed phyla, both simple and complex, appear simultaneously at the first, and continue without change into the present.

6) There are no transition fossils between the simpler and the more complex forms of life.

7) There is no evidence of any change of a life form from one phylum into another.

8) The doctrine of "emergence", that evolution allows the sudden appearance of new forms without relation to previous forms, is required.

9) Instead of "missing links" there is really a missing chain.

10) There is no theory of a mechanism that is adequate.

11) There is no allowance for purpose or design in the universe. Everything is meaningless.

12) Biological evolution has stopped. Man is as high as evolution will ever go. Any future development will be in the realm of culture and ideas.

RECENT CLAIMS

We are all aware that there are continuing "new releases" found in the media of certain "finds" that lay claim to being new evidence in support of evolution — perhaps a new, possible "missing link" or a new "confirmation" of the theory in some way. Concerning these we should be aware that scientists are people like the rest of us, some of whom would enjoy seeing their names or articles in the paper, and we should also be aware that the media people are not scholars, qualified to pass authoritative judgment on such matters. Unfortunately, too, many of the rest of us are credulous, and will accept at face value anything that gets into print.

What we are saying is that before anything this important is believed we should know that top scholars from several different philosophical stances have studied and evaluated the claim. There have been numerous hoaxes, e.g., the Piltdown man, and therefore, it is a fair warning for us to question anything that appears in the public media. Normally scholars and technical experts first print their findings with supporting evidence in the scholarly journals.

Again, we often find unqualified editors and columnists pontificating, especially about evolution, and this is done largely on the basis of the public's general acceptance of its truth. Lawsuits and court trials make headlines, and, since many scientists are committed to the philosophy of naturalism their voices are frequently given undue authority. The great need is for the factual truth to be known, as we have attempted to set forth in this volume.

A BATTLE OF ULTIMATES

The entire question concerning the theory of evolution is really a battle of ultimates — one of God versus chance-process in nature. It is a battle of purpose and meaning to human existence against the idea that the world and life are meaningless.

There is no reason why people who have faith in God should accept naturalistic conclusions. If God has power to create the spirit of man and place it in a ready-made body, he would have power to create the body also, even instantaneously, had he seen fit. Indeed, a powerful God is not limited to natural law as his mode of operation. Certainly he can use nature or natural law for any of his purposes, but his revelation in the Bible does not indicate that he did use a process of naturalistic evolution to produce man. After all, he is the author of nature, and can use it or "go around it" as he sees fit. The Bible clearly states that man and woman were made by special acts of creation, but this is no problem to a God who is above nature.

The facts of science and the laws of nature insist that "life comes only from life," and "something does not come from nothing." Spontaneous generation of life is contrary to what we know from science and from the laws of nature.

CREATION SCIENCE

There is a group who are strongly committed to opposing the teaching of evolution, and who operate under the designation of "Creation Science." We suppose that the choice of this term is a hope of dignifying their efforts as being just as truly scientific as their opposition. We agree with many of their conclusions, but it would seem that they chose an unhappy term in claiming that "science" supports their faith. They apparently wanted to tell the world that they are as scientific as the evolutionists, and indeed this is true, because science doesn't prove evolution, neither does it disprove it, as we have shown. Neither side of the argument about evolution is able, therefore, to depend upon scientific proof, for there is none. Both sides have to use faith to arrive at the conclusions they do. The "Creation Science" people, though, are at a disadvantage because they want to use the word "science," when their opposition are known as "scientists" and they are commonly known as religionists. Indeed, their arguments fit in with what science has actually proved just the same as it can square with some of the things the evolutionists argue for. The facts are, however, that evolution is NOT provable by science, nor is it disprovable by science. It is a philosophical question, and conclusions are reached by faith.

THE OUTLOOK OF CHRISTIAN FAITH

What, then, should a Christian believe about all the issues and arguments concerning evolution? He should believe in God, in Christ and the Bible, but he should realize that his faith is not dependent upon how old the universe is, or how old the earth is. The fact of creation is absolute and clear. How it was all accomplished is not an issue for Christian faith. The Bible is not a scientific textbook and one can have a valid faith in God as the Creator without even having to consider all these other matters.

The Bible is clear enough and specific enough on what is important for a person to believe. To believe in Jesus Christ as God's Son and our Saviour is easily understood. There is no question about whether we should commit to his will and obey it. To live a faithful, moral life as free from sin as possible and to depend upon God's grace for forgiveness for our failures, are all things that are clearly taught and understandable.

The end of the matter; all has been heard. Fear God, and keep his commandments; for this is the whole duty of man. For God will bring every deed into judgment, with every secret thing, whether good or evil. —ECCLESIASTES 12:13,14

N O T E S

1. Spengler, Oswald, *The Decline of the West*, Vol.II, New York: Knopf, 1932, p.32.

2. Shapley, Harlow, Panel I,"The Origin of Life," in *Evolution After Darwin,,* Vol.III, *Issues In Evolution*, Chicago: Univ. of Chicago Press,

APPENDIX

JOHN N. CLAYTON

A little boy was aked by a minister why he believed in God. He replied, "I guess it's been in our family for a long time." Unfortunately, that answer is the reason many of us hold to the religious convictions that we have. We really do not know why we believe what we believe; we have simply accepted the traditions of our childhood and are following that acceptance through life. I, too, accepted the traditions of my childhood; but, unlike many people, my belief system was one of atheism. My memory of religious statements by my parents and many of their associates involve things like:

"Do you really believe there's an 'Old Man' up in the sky zapping things into existence here upon the earth?"

"Do you really believe that the church makes any difference in what people do?"

"How can anyone believe all that 'mumbo jumbo' that preachers preach?"

By the time I was 8 years old, I had accepted the notion that only foolish, ignorant, uneducated people believed in God. As

I moved into adolescence, I became increasingly active in atheism. As my science education accelerated, I became more and more committed to the idea that science and technology held the keys to solving man's problems. By the time I was 16 years old, I was a hard-core, aggressive atheist, attacking anything that smacked of religion in any way.

Late in my high school career, I had the fortune to take a physics class under a teacher named Mr. Gross, whom I had grown to respect from my contact with him in the 8th grade. Unlike the 8th grade class, however, the physics class had laboratory periods when a student could talk to the teacher and get to know him. My caustic remarks about God and the Bible were always met with a warm smile by Mr. Gross, but never a response. One day after an especially biting remark from me about "the stupidity of religion and the Bible," he asked me if I had ever studied the scientific accuracy of the Bible. I had never even read the Bible, much less studied it, so I had to answer negatively. He said, "You know, John, I had a terrible time trying to decide whether to become a teacher or a preacher. I finally decided that God speaks as well in His creation as He does in the Bible and the two agree exactly. I suggest that you study both. Start with Genesis.."

I was shocked to learn that this man whom I respected as a scientist would be a believer in God, much less that he had considered becoming a minister. I was even more appalled that he would suggest that Genesis 1 and science would agree. All my life, I had heard that the Biblical account was a lot of foolishness and myth that no logical person could accept. If Genesis were myth, it could not be scientifically accurate. In addition to this stimulus from Mr. Gross, I had a young lady friend who was encouraging me to read the Bible. She was a Christian who attended the services of the church regularly. We had been dating two years or so, and I suspected that I was in love with her. She was a moral giant, uncompromising in her beliefs, and confident about her faith. When arguments came up, she always reverted to the Bible as the basis of her decisions. I decided that, if I could prove the Bible wrong, I could win a lot of arguments with her as well as prove to myself that Mr. Gross was wrong. So, I decided to study the first chapter of Genesis in detail. I was sure that with the knowledge of geology and evolution that I had gained by that time, I could easily destroy any credibility the Bible might have. My parents had told me that the Genesis record gave many teachings which modern science had proven to be false. I was so sure about the ease with which I could destroy anyone's belief in the integrity of the Genesis record that I decided to take exhaustive notes and write a book which I would title *All the Stupidity of the Bible*. Now I could add the making of money to the motivations I had to prove the Bible wrong.

Armed with this truck load of prejudice, dictionaries, and a dozen or so books on geology and evolution, I began my personal annihilation of the Genesis account of creation. Having never attended a Bible class, and not having heard a sermon, would turn out to be an advantage for me, for I had no preconceived ideas about what the Genesis record taught.

My first surprise came in the very first verse of Genesis 1. When I read, "In the beginning God created the heaven and the earth," I realized that this first verse dealt with a subject to which evolution could not address itself — creation. As an atheist, it had never occurred to me that evolution *assumed* everything. Genesis 1:1 states — that matter exists and it exists in a way that could produce and sustain life. Evolution does not deal with creation. It only deals with how things may have changed once they were already created.

I dislike the term "creation science" when that term is applied to rebuttals of theories of evolution. The creation of the cosmos "out of nothing" is creation. Hypothetical models of how living things may have changed from one form to another is *not* creation!

My second surprise in reading Genesis 1:1 was that it was not dated. I had always been told that the Biblical record taught that the earth was created in the year 4004 B.C. To maintain such a position, every verse in the Genesis record had to be dated. This first verse was not dated. It also was not stated as a summary verse, but as an historical event. The verse doesn't say that the next 28 verses are explaining what the first verse says. "In the beginning God created. . . ." is an event. Something took place. It is not an introduction to duplicate statements in later verses. As I continued reading through the early part of Genesis 1, I read about other conditions on the earth which I knew were essential to the development of life. The atmosphere, water, land and all the other conditions needed for life were described. I became uneasy as I saw this careful and accurate description, but I was still confident that the evolution of life would ultimately expose the fallacious nature of the Bible's history.

At verses 10 and 11, I came in contact with the first description of life on the earth. In my studies in science, I had learned that the first living thing on the earth was a plant. It was logical that an organism which could turn sunlight into food was necessary for the origination of life. In addition to this logic, I had seen plant fossils and had studied the sequence that plants follow in populating a barren area whether it be on land or in the sea. I knew that simple plants like algae or lichen are followed by gymnosperms (ferns and conifers), which are followed by angiosperms (seed plants like dogwood or apple trees). Imagine my surprise when I found Genesis giving exactly the same sequence!

"God said, Let the earth bring forth grass. . . ." The Hebrew word *deshe* is used here, indicating moss or algae or lichen.

204

The word *catshir* is not used, which is the kind of grass on which one uses a lawnmower. The second kind of plant was "the herb" from the Hebrew word *eseb*. This word is used when referring to the kind of plants science calls "gymnosperms." The most recent kind of plant, according to Genesis, was the flowering "tree-yielding fruit." What better description could be given of the succession I knew to be a modern concept of science. How could the ancient writer of Genesis have accurately described the logical sequence in which plants were created?

In verse 20, I was to receive more surprises. The Biblical record identifies the first animal to appear upon the earth. The statement was clear and, for the first time, I thought I had something in the Bible I could prove to be wrong. "And God said, Let the waters bring forth abundantly the moving creature that hath life...." Clearly the indication was that the first animals upon the earth were water creatures. That point could not be argued. The trilobite and other marine fossils have strongly testified that animal life began in the sea. The Genesis account indicated that many forms of sea life came into existence at the same time. In my biology classes, I had been taught that life began as simple animals and gradually evolved to more complex animals. I had drawn models of how the sponges might have evolved into corals and how the various molluscs might have led to higher forms of life. I had also been told that backboned (*vertebrate*) animals were very recent additions to the earth's life forms compared to the trilobite and its friends.

I was elated at this obvious conflict between the Biblical record and the facts, and I rushed to the geology library to get pictures to document the facts. As I studied the listings of fossils and their ages and classifications, I found Cambrian fossils (the geologic period at the beginning of life on earth) which were extremely advanced. The graptolite was a fossil which was very abundant in the fossil record of the Cambrian period; but the graptolite was classified as a vertebrate. The acorn worm and lancelot were other Cambrian fossils which were vertebrates. In no way did the fossil record verify the transitions that I had always had presented to me. I returned to Genesis 1:20 and received another blow to my confidence in evolutionary theory.

One of the models used in evolution is the model of the evolution of the bird. The theory has usually been that the first birds were walking birds like an ostrich. The idea is that the breastbone, wing muscles, feathers, and hollow bones would have to develop gradually over long periods of time. The idea then was that flight evolved. Good flyers would be the more recent birds, and the first birds would have been non-flyers or poor flyers. In Genesis 1:20-21, we are told that the "winged fowl" became abundant "in the open firmament of heaven." Once again, I was confident that this Biblical assertion that the first birds were flying birds could be proven to be wrong. And, once again, a visit to the geological library proved the Bible to be right. Today the earliest known bird is called "protoavis." It is a bird that could fly beautifully. All of the equipment needed for flight is there, in advanced form. The archaeopteryx, a fossil of more recent age, is also capable of flight and possesses feathers and bone structures designed for use in the air.

As I continued to read Genesis, I found that mammals were the next living things to come into existence on the earth. The most recent thing to appear on the earth, according to Genesis, was man. Once again I could offer no criticism. The fossil record supports this sequence of life beautifully. I could not find a single statement in the Genesis account that I could prove to be in error. There were many things that the Bible did not explain, but everything it did say was correct. Amoebas, viruses, platypuses, echidas, walking and swimming birds, and a myriad of other life forms were not included in the account, but what was described was correct. Many questions about "time" remained unanswered because they were not germane to the Bible's message that God created all things.

All this destruction of my prejudices about the Bible led me next to question further what I had been told about the theory of evolution. It was obvious that *change* was a working agent in creation, and that this type of *change* could in a sense be called "evolution." New breeds of dogs, cattle, roses, cats, etc., are not alien to the Bible. Jacob used this kind of change in manipulating Laban's cattle. The fact that all races of men on the earth are descendants of Eve (whose name means "the mother of all living"), further demonstrates that evolution (minor changes) takes place.

The question, then, is whether evolution can explain the existence of 20th century man in terms of "natural, chance modifications of an original amoeba." My faith in evolution had been shaken by my Biblical confrontation; so now I wanted real proof that the evolution of man from an original amoeba was true. By this time I was in college. My training in science was advancing rapidly. During my sophomore year at Indiana University, I enrolled in a geology course taught by a well-known atheist. He began the class by holding up a Bible and stating "I'm going to show you that this (the Bible) is a bunch of garbage." This was my golden opportunity to get the proof of evolution that I desired, and so I tore into the text and the course with enthusiasm and anticipation. My joy in anticipating this newly-found hope of information was short-lived. As we studied the fossil record, we were given sheets of paper showing evolutionary sequences from one form of life to another. When we studied the evolution of mammals from the reptiles, we were shown a fossil which was obvious to me to be an alligator skeleton. Written on the specimen was the term, "therapsid — mammal-like reptile." For nearly an hour, I studied the fossil, unable to find anything in it that was mammalian in nature. The therapsid is supposed to be "the best of the transition fossils" between major groups of living things. I finally went to the professor and told him that I could find nothing mammalian about the fossil. He pointed to a small bone in the inner ear and another small bone in the lower jaw and said, "These two bones are mammal-like." As I looked at the specimen next to mine, I saw that the bones were somewhat different from those in my specimen. When I asked about this difference, I was told that they were just variations between individuals. It was obvious to me that some choosing was being done here about which variations would be considered and which should be ignored. "Is this really the best transition fossil we can see?" I asked, referring to the therapsid. I was assured that it was.

In the class, we learned other things that I could not fit in with evolution. We learned that evolution is dependent upon the assumption that the earth has always functioned in a consistent way — that there have been no global catastrophes like the flood, which could have stopped evolution and made gradualism impossible. Even at that time, I had seen pictures of quickly frozen elephants and had seen huge meteor craters, both of which indicate that uniformitarianism in geology was a bad *assumption*. In the 1980s, there have been discoveries of asteroid material in stratified layers marking the mass extinctions of such animals as the dinosaurs. These discoveries have further supported catastrophism as an agent of change in the earth's history. It was becoming obvious to me that my faith in evolution as the explanation of how everything came to be was based on some bad assumptions.

My further study of Genesis and my experiences of life convinced me of one more Biblical truth which ultimately led me to become a Christian. That was the realization that man is not just an animal, as evolution would have us to believe, but he was rather a spiritual being — uniquely and specially created in the image of God! When the Bible writer tells us that we are created in God's image, it should be obvious that the Bible is not referring to our physical bodies. God is not a man, but a spirit (John 4:24). If we are all in God's image, we must all be alike, in some real sense. Obviously we are not alike physically, so it must be our spiritual nature that the Bible is here referring to. Even as an atheist, when I looked at man's creative ability in art and music, his ability to experience such emotions as guilt and sympathy and compassion, and man's desire and ability to worship, it was obvious that man was not just "a naked ape." When I discussed these characteristics with my anthropologist friends, I found them trying to explain them in terms of intelligence or environment. In my studies in psychology, I had seen that putting intelligent apes in human homes would not make them human. I also had seen severely retarded humans who could do all of these things. To try to explain all of man's unique characteristics in terms of intelligence or environment is to ignore mountains of scientific and educational data that show that man is a special and a spiritual being. Questions of morality and love cannot be answered in the framework of reducing man to a purely physical being. My life as an atheist was a life of alternating pleasure and misery. There had to be more to man's existence than what I had experienced and learned as an atheist.

I became a Christian because of the evidence available to support belief. My journey arrived at faith, which although it reaches beyond a certainty, is not near the "leap of faith" which the atheistic evolutionist has to take. My experience since my conversion to Jesus Christ has brought me to see that we live in a world where many want to believe, but the saturation of our world with bad theology and bad science has made belief difficult for many.

Let us speak to this frustrated world with both clarity and love, to come to God the Creator by studying both His Word and His Creation.

[Editor's Note: Although John N. Clayton is not a member of the ACU faculty, he has lectured three times on our campus against evolution. The time I was the "host" for his series he gave the preceding lecture to our students on his own conversion to Christ. I recall it as the "most spiritual" hour of my 33 years of teaching on the campus. Clayton has given his "Does God Exist" series in 750 congregations in the United States, Canada and England. They total about 7,500 presentations. At present he is scheduling about 40 Lectureships per year, or approximately 400 presentations. Fifteen or twenty colleges are included each year in his lecture series. and there are about 15,000 people enrolled in his Correspondence courses annually. He publishes a "Does God Exist?" journal which is mailed free. I know of no one who is personally fighting evolution and for faith in God and Christ more than John Clayton. May his tribe increase!]

PERSONALIA

ARLIE J. HOOVER

Arlie J. Hoover received the B.A. degree from the University of Tampa, in Florida, in 1960; the M.A. in 1962 and the Ph.D. in 1965, both in History and Philosophy and both from the University of Texas. He did doctoral research at the Free University of Berlin, in Germany, in 1963 and 1964, and post-doctoral research at the University of Heidelberg in Germany in 1968.

He has served as Professor of History at Pepperdine University, 1964-1977; as Academic Dean at Columbia Christian College, Portland, Oregon, 1977-1980; and has been a Professor of History at Abilene Christian University from 1980 to the present.

Dr. Hoover has had numerous awards — the Woodrow Wilson National Fellowship, 1960-61, University of Texas; a Fullbright Grant, Free University of Berlin, 1963-64; Exchange Fellowship, Univ. of Texas to Univ. of Berlin, 1963-64; three research grants — Heidelberg, 1968; Marburg, 1985; and Oxford, 1986. In 1972 and 1973 he was listed among the Outstanding Educators of America.

Hoover has published a large number of papers on German History and Philosophical thought, and has written a large number of books, many of which are in defense of Christian faith, and one which was chosen as a monthly selection be the Evangelical Book Club, *The Case For Christian Theism.* A recent volume is entitled, *The Case For Teaching Creation,* which shows his qualifications and interest in the present volume. He is extremely well qualified as a defender of Christian faith, having had several debates with atheists.

CHARLES FELIX

Charles Felix serves as Professor of Geology and Chairman of the Department at Abilene Christian University. He received his B.A. degree in Botany from the University of Tennessee and M.A. and Ph.D. degrees in Paleobotany from Washington University in St. Louis. He has also done postgraduate work at the University of Michigan and Southern Methodist University. Dr. Felix has served as Instructor in Botany at Washington University in St. Louis, as geologist for the United States Geological Survey, and over a period of 25 years he worked in a wide variety of supervisory positions with the Sun Oil Company as research geologist and exploration geologist. He joined the faculty of Abilene Christian University in 1981.

Dr. Felix is the author of 35 scientific publications and monographs in geology and paleontology, and his current research interests are primarily the paleontology of the Canadian Arctic polar regions and source bed geochemistry of organic rocks. He is a University Fellow of Washington University, a former National Science Scholar, and a member of the honor societies of Sigma Xi, Phi Kappa Phi, and Phi Beta Kappa. He is married to the formar June Ann Alsobrook of Loraine, Texas, and they are the parents of three daughters, all of whom attended Abilene Christian University.

JAMES R. NICHOLS

James R. Nichols was born in 1944 in Kansas City, Missouri, and grew up in the Kansas City area. He received the B.S. degree from Abilene Christian University in 1966, the M.S. from the University of Michigan at Ann Arbor in 1968, and the Ph.D. from the University of Missouri at Columbia in 1973.

He has served as a faculty member in the Biology department of the University of Central Arkansas, as a Fellow in the Department of Physiology at the University of Kansas Medical Center at Kansas City, as a Visiting Scientist/ Visiting Professor in the Medical Research Service of the Veterans Administration Hospital in Little Rock and at the Texas Tech University Health Sciences Center at Lubbock. He has been Professor of Biology at Abilene Christian University since 1982.

Dr. Nichols holds memberships in the American Institute of Biological Sciences, the American Society of Zoologists, and the American Association for the Advancement of Science. He serves on the Health Professions Advisory Committee. In 1987 Dr. Nichols received the Outstanding Professor Award for the College of Natural and Applied Sciences at ACU.

He is married to Jeanenne, a kindergarten teacher in the Abilene Public Schools, and they have three children, Amy, Joel, and Elizabeth. He is serving as a Deacon in the Minter Lane Church of Christ.

WM. CLARK STEVENS

Wm. Clark Stevens was born in Richland, Texas, in 1921 and graduated from high school there. After serving in the Army Air Corps during World War II, he graduated with the B.A. degree in Biology from Harding University in 1948. He received the Master's degree in Zoology from the University of

Arkansas in 1951, and the Ph.D. from Vanderbilt University in 1956.

Dr. Stevens was awarded a National Institutes of Health post-doctoral Fellowship in 1962 to Study Marine Biology for a year at the Marine Institute of the University of Miami. In 1974 he did special study in Diagnostic Virology at the Center For Disease Control in Atlanta, Georgia, and he also studied in a program concerning Diagnostic Microbiology in 1978 at the Texas State Laboratory at Austin.

He has taught at four different colleges and universities: Instructor of Science at Beebe Junior College in Arkansas; Instructor of Biology, Vanderbilt University; Professor of Biology at Harding University; and Professor of Biology at Abilene Christian University, where he also served as Chairman of the Department for eighteen years (1966-1984).

His present duties, in addition to full-time teaching, include serving as Chairman of the Health Professions Advisory Committee at ACU.

PERRY C. REEVES

Perry C. Reeves was born in Brady, Texas, November 9,1942. He attended public schools in Mason, Texas, and was graduated from high school there in 1961. He enrolled in Abilene Christian University and received the B.S. degree in Chemistry in 1965. In the summer of 1964 he served as an NSF Summer Research Participant in biochemistry at Oklahoma State University. He received the Ph.D, degree in Organic Chemistry from the University of Texas in 1969. He began his teaching as Assistant Professor of Chemistry at Southern Methodist University and in 1978 was promoted to the rank of Professor of Chemistry. He was voted by the student body at SMU as one of the Outstanding Professors in 1979.

Dr. Reeves returned to Abilene Christian University in 1980 and the following year became Dean of the College of Natural and Applied Sciences. In 1987 he returned to full-time teaching and research in the Chemistry Department. He is the author or co-author of over 35 articles that have been published in national and international scientific journals. Since 1970 he has received almost $240,000 in grant support for research in the area of transition metal-organometallic chemistry. During this period he has supervised eighteen undergraduate and nine graduate students, of whom four have gone on to earn Ph.D. degrees and seven the M.D. degree. Seven others are currently in medical or graduate school.

Dr. Reeves and his wife, Judy, have two children, Amy and Mark. They are members of the Hillcrest Church of Christ in Abilene where he serves as an elder.

MICHAEL E. SADLER

Michael E. Sadler was born May 18,1948. His education includes the B.A. from Texas Tech University in Science, the M.A. from Indiana University in 1974, and the Ph.D. in 1977 from the same University.

In 1980 he joined the Physics faculty at Abilene Christian University, after having spent several years as a Research Physicist at the Department of Physics at UCLA, in Los Angeles. He also has been a Research Assistant at the Cyclotron Facility at the University of Indiana, as well as a Course Instructor there. In the fall of 1986 he did research at the Meson Physics Facility of the Los Alamos National Laboratory in New Mexico. During this period he attended the Seventh International Symposium on High Energy Spin Physics and read a paper in Russian on "Measurement of Spin Observables in Pion-Nucleon Scattering at LAMPF."

Sadler is a member of the American Physical Society, and the American Association of Physics Teachers. He has received numerous academic awards, including High School Valedictorian, Department of Physics graduate student award for outstanding research at Indiana University, and the Sabbatical Participant Award (AWU) with matching grant from the Los Alamos National Laboratory, 1986, totalling $168,000, and covering three years' research. His other research awards, from the Department of Energy amount to over $268,000 with matching grants from the ACU Research Council. In 1983 he read a paper in Karlsruhe, West Germany, on Pion-Nucleon Scattering. He has written a large number of scholarly papers and has delivered numerous reports to scholarly societies, including the annual meetings of the American Physical Society.

JOE T. ATOR

Mr. Ator received the B.S. degree from Abilene Christian University in 1947, and the M.S. degree in 1950 from Texas Technological University. He attended several other schools also, including UCLA, the University of Texas, and U.S.Navy Training Schools. He has taken Post-Graduate courses in Electronics and Infrared Systems at UCLA and the University of Michigan.

The first part of his professional career includes work and achievements in numerous scientific activities — the development of: image velocity sensors for airborne camera systems; flame sensing devices for industrial furnace control systems; electro recording instruments; data recording systems, industrial computer control systems; automatic target recognition techniques.

He joined the Aerospace Corporation in 1966 where he was involved in several highly technical developments. In 1978 he became manager of the Fort Hood Solar Energy Project for the U.S. Department of Energy. He was later assigned to space-related projects, designing the Consolidated Space Operations Center at Colorado Springs, and involved in planning of Space Shuttle flight operations. Presently he is managing a joint study of the Aerospace Corporation and the MIT Lincoln Laboratories of a future space-based surveillance system.

Since 1967, Ator has served on the technical staff at Aerospace; as Adjunct Professor in Natural Science at Pepperdine University; and as a part-time faculty member of the Physics and Astronomy Depart at California State University at Northridge.

Ator'a honors and appointments include mention in the 1966 edition of American Men of Science; Elder in the Van Nuys Church of Christ since 1971; Advisory Board, Abilene Christian University, 1972; Board of Trustees, Abilene Christian University, 1984; and as a member of the Sensor Systems Technical Committee, American Institute of Aeronautics and Astronautics, 1987. He is the holder of three patents for scientic developments and has been a member of five professional societies. He has presented papers or speeches to more than a dozen professional organizations.

IAN A. FAIR

Dr. Ian A. Fair, a native of South Africa, received his B.A. degree from Abilene Christian University, and he received the B.A. (Hon.), the M.A. and the Ph.D. in New Testament and Systematic Theology from the University of Natal, South Africa.

Dr. Fair's ministry includes preaching and mission work in South Africa from 1960 to 1974. He established numerous congregations among both the white and black peoples of South Africa, and was responsible, with Tex Williams and

Delbert McCloud, for founding the Natal School of Preaching for the training of black ministers in South Africa. He was the Director of that school from 1968 - 1974, and he has also served as Chairman of the Board of Trustees of the South Africa Bible School in Benoni, South Africa. In America he served as Dean and Instructor at the Sunset School of Preaching in Lubbock, Texas, from 1974 - 1978, and since 1978 he has been at Abilene Christian University where he now serves as Dean of the College of the Bible, and as Professor of Bible.

His professional memberships and other fields of special interest include: South African Society for Missiological Studies from 1970-1976; the Society of Biblical Literature; the American Academy of Religion; the Southwest Biblical Seminar; the Seminar of the Development of Early Catholic Christianity; and the Evangelical Theological Society, all in America. Fields of teaching and research include The Synoptic Gospels, Romans, Revelation, Advanced Introduction to the New Testament, Contemporary Religious Thought, and Religious Teachings of the New Testament.

Ian is married to the former June Stent, and they have three sons, Deon (married to Susan Slaughter), Nigel, and Douglas (married to Joy Hulett); and there are two grandchildren, Rachel and Kevin, children of Deon and Susan.

NEIL R. LIGHTFOOT

Dr. Neil R. Lighfoot, a native of Waco, Texas, received the B.A. and the M.A. degrees in philosophy from Baylor University, and he later was granted the Ph.D. degree in New Testament by Duke University. He joined the Bible faculty at Abilene Christian University in 1958, where he now teaches New Testament, although he has formerly taught Biblical Languages (Greek and Hebrew), Apologetics and Evidences of Christianity.

Dr. Lightfoot has been active as a lecturer and preacher, having served as fulltime minister for several congregations in both North Carolina and Texas. He has preached for forty years and has served the Eleventh and Willis Church of Christ in Abilene as an elder for twenty years.

Dr. Lightfoot is well-known for his writings, which include books and articles as well as filmstrips. His books include: How *We Got the Bible* (recently revised), *Lessons From the Parables, Jesus Christ Today: A Commentary on the Book of Hebrews,* and *The Role of Women: New Testament Perspectives.* Filmstrips include: *How We Got The Bible, Now That I Am A Christian,* and *Can We Believe The Bible?* He has also served as Greek Text Editor and as one of the Translators of The International Children's Version (NT) and, The Word: The New Century Version (NT).

Awards and honors received include: "Trustee's Award: Outstanding Teacher of the Year" for 1978 at Abilene Christian University; Senior Associate, Westminster College, Cambridge University, Cambridge England, for 1985; and in 1987 Lightfoot was named Frank Pack Distinguished Professor of New Testament at Abilene Christian University.

JOHN C. CLAYTON

John C. Clayton was born in 1938. His B.S. degree in Education, with an emphasis in Physics and Math, was earned at Indiana University in 1959. An M.S. in Education, emphasizing Chemistry and Psychometry was awarded him by the same University in 1962. The M.S. in Geology and Earth Science was received from Notre Dame University in 1971.

He has taught in high schools in South Bend, Indiana from 1959 to the present, teaching General Science, Math, Chemistry, Physics, and Earth Science at different periods. He has also taught as a Professor of Education at St. Mary's College in South Bend and at Montana State University for the National Science Foundation..

Clayton has received several honors as a teacher, including : "Teacher of the Year" by the East Central Region of the National Association of Geology Teachers in 1972; "Best Teacher" award — selection by students of Riley High School in 1976; and "Distinguished Physics Teacher" for the State of Indiana - 1985, by the American Association of Physics Teachers.

His active memberships include: National Education Association; Indiana State Teachers Association; Council for the Retarded of St. Joseph County; National Science Teachers Association; Astronomy Teachers Association; American Association of Physics Teachers, and the American Scientific Affiliation.

Clayton's wife, Phyllis is a co-worker with him in all these activities, and it was primarily she who is responsible for his conversion. Their children include: Cathy, born in 1964, Wendy, born in 1967, and Tim, a multiple-handicapped child, who has been in the family since the age of 9 weeks (June 1962).

Perhaps Clayton's greatest work has been his "DOES GOD EXIST" lectureships, which together with his Correspondence courses, Audio-Tutorial Tapes and other religious education materials has taken him all over the nation the past 19 years. (See the introduction to his article in the appendix for more information on this).

J. D. THOMAS, EDITOR

J. D. Thomas is retired as Professor of Bible at Abilene Christian University, where he taught from 1949 to 1982. His training includes the B.A. in Bible and Greek from Abilene Christian, an M.A. in Church History from Southern Methodist University, and the Ph.D. from the Humanities Department of the University of Chicago in New Testament and Early Christian Literature.

His career includes service as Assistant City Manager at Lubbock, Texas, 1939-42; and as Minister for the Northwest Church of Christ in Chicago while attending the University there. He was Director of the Annual Bible Lectureship at ACU for 18 years, after which he served as Head of the Bible Department for nine years, until he retired. He served as Elder at the University Church of Christ for about 25 years.

Thomas is a member of the Corporation Board of the Restoration Quarterly, and has held memberships in the Society of Biblical Literature, (one time President of the Southwestern Section), the American Academy of Religion, The Southwestern Philosophical Society, the American Scientific Affiliation, and the Evangelical Theological Society. He has served on the Advisory Board of the American Bible Society, was in the 1970 edition of Outstanding Educators of America, several editions of Who's Who in the South and Southwest, and Who's Who in Religion, and was listed in the 38th edition of Who's Who in America.

As editor and publisher of Biblical Research Press, Thomas has published over eighty different books, 18 of which he wrote himself, and all of which are now owned by the ACU Press. The best known of his writings are probably *We Be Brethren, Facts and Faith, Divorce and Remarriage*, his brief commentary on Romans in the WAY of LIFE series, and a paperback on Evolution which has sold worldwide in four printings.

221

He was the 1958 speaker on the Far East Fellowship in Tokyo, Japan, and he and his wife did a four month around-the-world tour in 1969, visiting missionaries in thirty different countries, and during which he spoke 132 times, and they visited with thirty six of his own former students. His wife is the former Mary Katherine Payne. They had three children, Deborah (now deceased), Hannah and John Paul, all of whom graduated from Abilene Christian.

GLOSSARY

Alphabetic Writing — Man's most advanced form of writing (uses the fewest characters). Began about the 18th Century B.C.

Authority — One in position of having empirical knowledge, who testifies or reveals information to another, who then accepts it as truth by faith or assent.

Big Bang — Theory that all matter in the universe had a common origin in both space and time. The "expanding universe" is therefore roughly datable as to its origin. Clearly infers a "beginning."

Biogenetic Law — Same as the theory of recapitulation, that "Ontogeny recapitulates phylogeny." An embryo goes through all the evolutionary stages in its development.

Cambrian — The geological period about 500 or so million years ago, at which level the earliest fossils appear, already separated into distinct phyla.

Catastrophe — Term that describes a geologic upheaval, such as may have been caused by the Flood, Plate Tectonics or similar force. Catastrophes are thought by some to have caused the present geological strata, fossil deposits, etc.

Catastrophism — The philosophy that a series of catastrophes in nature is responsible for the present geological structures of the earth.

Change — A recognition that changes in organisms do occur within the minor groupings of the taxa. No real changes are known among the major groupings, however.

Classes — Second major group, next to phyla, in the usual taxonomic list.

Comparative Anatomy — Comparison of body structures of various organisms. Theory that similarity meant a common evolutionary descent.

Comparative Embryology — A study similar in interest and purpose to Comparative Anatomy, except that it is limited to embryos.

Continuous Creation — Same as the "Steady State Theory." Assumes that new matter is constantly being created to fill the void left by the expanding universe. Seeks to prove an "eternal" universe.

Creation — View that God created the universe and all that is in it by "fiat" decree.

Day (s) — One (or more) of the "days" of creation. Various theories about the lengths of these days.

Determinism — Philosophy that mind cannot control or change events. All that happens is pre-determined by some cosmic force.

Emergent Evolution — A term arbitrarily applied to the sudden appearance of newer and higher forms of life that appear in the fossil record, without evidence of their having come from any former organisms, so that the process can still be called "evolution."

Empiricism (Adjective - Empirical) — The use of the five senses; the view that factual knowledge comes through empirical observation, and is therefore a more certain knowledge than that received by reason or the testimony of others.

Evolution — The philosophy that all life came from very simple original life-forms, by natural process only. (See General Theory of Evolution; also see Macro-evolution) .

Expanding Universe — Theory that the universe was originally compact, but has been expanding at a constant rate. The rate is measurable and thus a date for the original creation can be established.

External Authority — Authority that is external to man himself, such as God, or his word, the Bible.

Extrapolation — To apply knowledge in a known area to an unknown area, assuming that it works there equally well. In our study, to assume that changes among the minor groupings of the taxa prove that changes in the major groupings have occurred by the same processes.

Fact — A working hypothesis detrermined by the scientific method. Illustrations could be the Salk vaccine; and the fact that water is composed of H_2O.

Faith — A commitment that is not based upon scientific fact, but goes beyond empirical knowledge.

Families — The fourth member of the taxonomic classification. Phyla, Classes, Orders, Families.

Fixity of the Species — Term that indicates that organisms are "fixed," in the sense that no changes of body structures ever occur. Not true of the lower taxonomic groups but believed to be true of the major groups.

Fossil — Skeletons or other structural remains or impressions of organisms that are found in geological formations in the earth's crust.

Fossil Record — The total information gleaned from fossil finds.

Gap, Gap Theory — Possible period of time during the chaotic condition of Genesis 1:2. (The possibility of fossils being assigned to such a period).

Genera (Singular - Genus) — The fifth grouping (of six) in the taxonomic list. "Species" is number six.

General Theory of Evolution — The real theory of evolution opposed by creationists. Same as Macroevolution, the "amoeba to man" view.

Geocentric Syatem — View of our solar system where the earth is the center and main planet, with all revolving about it.

Geologic Time-Table — The geologic "calender," called the cornerstone of geology. It portrays the rock units of the earth in an orderly arrangement, from the oldest to the youngest, with the fossils arrranged in an orderly evolutionary sequence. It is an assumption, based upon uniformitarian philosophy.

Geology — A study of the history of the earth and its crust, especially its rock formations.

Genetic Code — The chemical pattern of information which determines the inheritable characteristics of the cell, and thus the individual. Extremely complex.

Gradualism — Darwin's thesis, that evolutionary development was slow and required a long time. Now being replaced by the "punctuated equilibrium" theory.

Half-Life — The time required for one half of the original strength of a radioactive element to disseminate. Different times are required for different elements. Carbon requires about 5700 years.

Heliocentric System — View of the solar system where the sun is the central planet and all revolves about it.

Homologous Organs — Similar organs in different organisms, as a man's arm; a bird's wing, a whale's flipper, etc.

Hubble's Law — The thesis that the distances of stars and galaxies correlate with the velocity at which they are receding. This principle enables the measurement of the age of the universe, based upon the assumption that the velocities have been constant.

Inference — Basis for judgment that is less than direct observation. Uses circumstantial evidence, and approaches events indirectly. Its conclusions are in the "loose science" category.

Isotope — Technically, they are nuclei which have the same electronic charge but different masses. More simply, they are unstable nuclei because of radioactive emanations. "Normal" carbon, for instance is ^{12}C, while radioactive carbon is ^{14}C.

Light-year — Distance light can travel in a year at 286,00 miles per second.

Loose Science — Conclusions that do not have the benefit of direct observation in obtaining data, and therefore must rely upon inference, circumstantial evidence, and indirect information for data upon which to base its conclusions. Lacks certainty. Not "factual."

Macroevolution — Same as the General Theory of Evolution. Literally "Big Evolution." From "scratch" on up to man.

Materialism — Philosophy that everything is matter. A denial of anything spiritual or metaphysical.

Mechanism (of evolution) — The supposed methodology of "how" evolution happened, that is, how lower forms naturally produced the higher forms of life (from "scratch" on up to man).

Metaphysical — That realm of reality which lies beyond the physical. Embraces the spiritual, the mental, abstract things, and values, such as good and bad, and right and wrong.

Microevolution — Minor changes in organisms, which are known in species and perhaps in genera, but not in the major groupings of the taxa.

Morality — A value, namely, that good is more valuable than bad; and right is more valuable than wrong.

Mutation — A change, chemical or otherwise, in a living form that is inheritable.

Naturalism — Philosophy that holds that Nature is the ultimate reality and ultimate power in the universe. Denies supernaturalism, as God and spirit.

Natural Selection — Darwin's explanation of one aspect of his theory of evolutionary mechanism.

Observation — The empirical experiences upon which science is based. It comes through one or more of the five senses and is therefore the most certain knowledge that man can arrive at.

Ockham's Razor — The philosophical claim that the simplest explanation of a problem is the correct one. Used widely by lawyers in circumstantial evidence trials.

Orders — The third major grouping in the taxonomic list. See Taxonomy.

Organic Evolution — Earlier designation for Macroevolution.

Organism — Life-form. A creature that has life at some time.

Origins — The concern with the beginnings and the source: of the universe, the earth, living creatures, and man.

Oscillation Theory — Theory that the universe, instead of expanding, or maintaining a "steady state," is oscillating, that is, continually expand for a time, then contracts for a time.

Paleontology — The study of past geological periods as determined from fossil remains.

Phenomenon (Plural - Phenomena) — An observable fact or event. Known through the senses rather than by thought or intuition.

Philosophy — 1) One's total worldview. 2) Speculative human thought, distinct from revelation.

Phyla (singular - phylum) — The largest grouping of animal life in the taxa. They are ten to thirty in number, and include all animals.

Plate Tectonics — Theory that the earth's crust is a brittle shell consisting of large land masses (plates), which move on an underlying, semi-molten, plastic layer.

Precambrian — The very earliest fossils were once thought to have appeared in the Cambrian geological period, but now a few have been found in the late Precambrian period.

Punctuated Equilibrium — Recent name given to the fact that evolution is no longer claimed to be gradual, but comes in "bursts" or sudden appearance of new life forms, with lengthy periods of "equilibrium," when no new forms appear.

Radioactive "Clock" — Radioactive element that emanates energy at a measurable rate, and can therefore be used in determining ancient datings.

Rationalism — 1) Philosophy that holds that reason is the only valid avenue of knowledge. 2) The process of rationalizing or reasoning.

Reality — Something which has the state of being real. A philosophical problem.

Recapitulation — In our study, the theory that an embryo goes through the entire evolutionary cycle during the period of its gestation.

Reconstruction (or Reconstitution) Theory — Same as the Gap Theory or the "Long Chaos" Theory.

Recombination — One of the changes that can occur in the structure of organisms, caused by the physical rearrangement of genes on chromosomes.

Reductionism — The logical fallacy of selecting a portion of a complex entity and then saying that the whole is merely that portion.

Relativism — Philosophy that argues against any absolutes. In morality, for example, every event is relative. Each person is his own authority. There is no absolute, public truth.

Reproductive Isolation — In speciation, separation for a time may contribute to the later inability of individuals to interbreed.

Science — Knowledge learned by empirical observation.

Scientific Method — Inductive reasoning, from the particular to the general, and emphasizing precise observation and the use of higher mathematics. Conclusions are "facts," hopefully.

Scientific Theory — A hypothesis that has not been demonstrated, and perhaps cannot be.

Scientism — Philosophical attitude which holds that science has access to all knowledge, and therefore ought to be used in all investigation. Nothing is knowable unless approved by science.

Second Law of Thermodynamics — Accepted scientific fact that radiant energy is being constantly disseminated, as in radioactive emanations, without any recharging process in nature. "The universe is running down."

Special Pleading — The logical fallacy of dramatizing the material that favors your position and ignoring or belittling that which does not.

Speciation — The inheritable changes that occur within a species or minor grouping of the taxa, where the changes are adequate to produce a non-interbreeding new species. Not known to apply to phyla or major groupings of the taxa.

Species — The most minor taxonomic grouping within a phylum. There are a million or more as now classified.

Spontaneous Generation — The theory that life sprang spontaneously (and naturally) from non-life without the benefit of a Creator.

Steady State Theory — An effort to claim an eternal universe by arguing for continuous creation (q.v.).

"Stellar Evolution" — The changes that take place in stars, including "star death."

Strict Science — Scientific knowledge where that data employed were determined by empirical observation, and therefore is factual and certain.

Subjective — Reality as perceived by the mind (thought or intuition) rather than by direct, empirical observation.

Supernatural — Existence of realities above or beyond the visible, observable universe. Recognition of the spiritual world as real.

Supernovae — Stars that have sudden increases in the intensity of their emission of light.

Survival of the Fittest — Darwin's term that furnished one part of his theory of the mechanism of evolution. The other was "natural selection."

Taxa (singular - taxon) — A taxanomic group or entity.

Taxonomy — The study of the classification of plants and animals according to their presumed natural relationships.

Theistic Evolution — Theory that man's body was developed over a long period while he was but a mere animal. God later infused the animal body with a soul to make it human.

Transitional Fossils — Theoretical life-forms between "mature" or fully-developed forms of the various organisms. A lengthy search has produced none.

Uniformitarianism — Theory, that all geological formations were slowly and uniformly laid down by the same processes that operate today. "The present is the key to the past." No catastrophes.

Values — In our study, those realities that are not empirically knowable, but yet are real. They may consist of abstract qualities as love, goodness, morality, happiness, etc., and also the opposites of these.

Variations — The same as "Changes." Known developments within the minor groupings of the taxa. Not known in the phyla, classes or orders.

Vertebrates — Organisms that have a spine or backbone.

Vestigial Organs — Rudimentary structures in an organism that has no known function. Supposedly they are evolutionary traces of ancestral organs that did have useful functions.

Worldview — One's total world outlook. What is reality and what the universe and its relations consist of.

INDEX